Joseph Priestley

A Letter to the Rev. Mr. John Palmer

In Defence of the Illustrations of Philosophical Necessity

Joseph Priestley

A Letter to the Rev. Mr. John Palmer
In Defence of the Illustrations of Philosophical Necessity

ISBN/EAN: 9783744764629

Printed in Europe, USA, Canada, Australia, Japan

Cover: Foto ©Thomas Meinert / pixelio.de

More available books at **www.hansebooks.com**

A LETTER

TO

The Rev. Mr. JOHN PALMER,

IN DEFENCE OF THE

Illustrations of Philosophical Necessity.

BY

JOSEPH PRIESTLEY, LL.D. F.R.S.

> Respecting Man, whatever wrong we call
> May, must be right, as relative to all.
>
> POPE.

BATH: PRINTED BY R. CRUTTWELL;
AND SOLD BY
J. JOHNSON, No. 72, ST. PAUL'S CHURCH-YARD, LONDON.
MDCCLXXIX.

Price One Shilling and Six-Pence.

To the Rev. Mr. PALMER.

DEAR SIR,

NOTWITHSTANDING my unwillingness to engage any farther in metaphysical controversy, there are some circumstances attending your *Observations on my Treatise on Philosophical Necessity*, that make me in this case less averse to it. You are an old acquaintance, whom I respect, and whom I believe to be actuated by the best views; you are thought to be a master of this subject, and have certainly given very particular attention to it; thinking, as I myself do, that it it is of the greatest importance; and now, in a work of considerable extent, you confine your observations to it.

Your publication has also been a work of great expectation among our common friends, who were apprized of your intentions. By your own account, in your Preface, it must have been composed more than a year ago. In this time it has been submitted to the perusal of persons of great learning and worth, who, I am informed, think highly of it, and have recommended the publication, not only as excellent in itself, but as very proper to follow that of Dr. Price, who was thought by them to have been too tender of me, in our amicable discussion, and to have made some imprudent concessions. Your work, it is thought, will supply the deficiency in his.

You had the generosity to propose submitting your work to my own private perusal; and though, for reasons of delicacy and propriety,

priety, I thought proper to decline it, I encouraged you in your design of publication. Also, though I did not, I believe, make you any particular promise, you will probably expect that, all things considered, I shall give you an answer. I therefore do it, and with the same freedom with which you yourself have written. But, I shall confine myself chiefly to the discussion of those points on which the real *merits of the question* turn, without replying at large to what you have advanced with respect to the *consequences* of the doctrine. Indeed, if the doctrine itself be true, we must take all the genuine consequences, whether we relish them or not. I proceed, therefore, to a state of the controversy between us, and the consideration of the nature and weight of what you urge with respect to it.

The principal argument for the doctrine of Necessity is briefly this: If, in two precisely equal situations of mind, with respect both to disposition and motives, two different determinations

minations of the will be possible, one of them must be an effect without a cause. Consequently, only one of them is possible.

Now all that the ingenuity of man can reply to this is, either that, though the determination be uncertain, or contingent (depending neither upon the previous disposition of mind, nor the motives presented to it) it will still, on some account or other, not properly be *an effect without a cause*. For that there can be any effect without a cause, no advocate for the doctrine of liberty has, I believe, ever asserted. Or, in the next place, it may be said, that the above is not a fair stating of the question in debate; for that the determinations may be invariably the same in the same circumstances, being agreeable to some constant law or rule, and yet, not being *necessarily* so, the necessarian, in fact, gains no advantage by the concession.

You, Sir, have combated the necessarians on both these grounds; maintaining that whatever

ever be the state of mind, or the motives present to it, it has within itself a power of determining without any regard to them, the *self-determining power* being itself the proper *cause* of the determination. You likewise assert that, though there should be the greatest *certainty* in all the determinations of the will, yet because it is not a *physical,* but only a *moral certainty,* it is not a proper *necessity.* I shall consider distinctly what you have advanced on both these views of the subject, in the order in which I have mentioned them.

SECTION I.

Of the Argument for the Doctrine of Necessity from the Consideration of the Nature of Cause and Effect.

"IN the very same circumstances," you say, p. 17, "in which the choice or determination was directed to one object of pursuit, it might have brought itself to will, or determine on the pursuit of a different, or contrary one. In other words, the mind is free to deliberate upon, and, in consequence of this, to chuse, and determine the motives of its conduct."

This state of the case, I would observe in the first place, evidently implies that the mind cannot determine itself without some motive; but you think that, because it is capable of

deliberating

deliberating upon motives, it can chuse what motive it will be determined by. But if the mind cannot finally determine without a motive, neither, surely, can it *deliberate*, that is, *determine to deliberate*, without a motive. Because the volition to deliberate cannot be of a different nature from the volition that is consequent to the deliberation. A volition, or a decision of the mind, by whatever name it be denominated, or whatever be its nature, must be one and the same thing. It must, in all cases, be subject to the same rule, if it be subject to rule, or else be equally subject to no rule at all. You had better, therefore, say at once, that every determination of the mind, even the final one, may proceed on no motive at all. And your next retreat will equally serve you here: for you still maintain that, though there be nothing, either in the disposition of mind, or the motives present to it, that was at all the cause of the determination, it will not be an effect without a cause, because the self-determining power is, itself, a proper and adequate cause.

" There

"There remains a proper cause," you say, "p. 24, a sufficient and adequate cause, for every volition or determination which is formed. This cause is that self-determining power, which is essential to agency, and in the exercise of which motion begins." Again, p. 36, "One principle of freedom in the human mind will sufficiently account for all their actions, and to seek after other causes, must, therefore, in his own way of reasoning, be wholly unnecessary."

Now to every thing that can be advanced to this purpose, I think I have given a satisfactory reply in the *additional illustrations*, printed in my *Correspondence with Dr. Price*, p. 288, in which I shew that the self-determining power, bearing an equal relation to any two different decisions, cannot be said to be a proper and adequate cause with respect to them both. But this section, I suppose, you must have overlooked, otherwise you could not but have thought it peculiarly necessary to reply to my observations on that subject,

subject, which so very materially affect your argument. I must, therefore, take the liberty to request that you would consider it, and reply to it.

To argue as you do here, in any other case, would be thought very extraordinary. If I ask the cause of what is called the *wind*, it is a sufficient answer to say, in the first instance, that it is caused by the motion of the air, and this by its partial rarefaction, &c. &c. &c.; but if I ask why it blows *north* rather than *south*, will it be sufficient to say that, *this* is caused by the motion of the air? The motion of the air being equally concerned in north and south winds, can never be deemed an adequate cause of one of them in preference to the other.

In like manner, the self-determining power, allowing that man has such a thing, and that it may be the cause of determining in general, can never be deemed a sufficient cause of any one particular determination, in preference to another.

another. Suppofing, therefore, two determinations to be poffible, and there be nothing but the mere felf-determining power to decide between them, the difpofition of mind and motives being all exactly equal, one of them muft want a proper caufe, juft as much as the north or the fouth wind would be without a proper caufe, if nothing could be affigned but the motion of the air in general, without fomething to determine why it fhould move this way rather than that.

Befides, abftractedly and ftrictly fpeaking, no *mere power* can ever be faid to be an adequate caufe of its own acts. It is true that no effect can be produced without a power capable of producing it; but power, univerfally, requires both *objects* and proper *circumftances*. What, for inftance, can be done with a *power of burning*, without fomething to burn, and this being placed within its fphere of action? What is a *power of thinking*, or *judging*, without ideas, or objects, to think and form a judgment upon? What, therefore,

fore, can be done with a power of *willing*, without something to call it forth? and it is impossible to state any case in which it can be *called forth*, without implying such *circumstances*, as will come under the description of *motives*, or *reasons* for its being exerted one way rather than another, exactly similar to any other power, that is, *power universally and abstractedly considered*, corporeal or intellectual, &c. &c. &c.

SECTION II.

How far the Arguments for the Doctrine of Necessity are affected by the Consideration of the Soul being material or immaterial.

BUT you have another resource besides that which I have considered in the preceding section; which is, that though it be true that, supposing the soul to be *material*, and subject to physical laws, every determination requires a foreign cause, yet if the soul be *immaterial*,

material, no such cause is necessary. It may then determine itself in whatever manner it pleases.

"The whole of it" (viz. the section concerning the argument from cause and effect) you say, p. 20, "supposes a similarity in the "constituent principles of matter and spirit; "for by those only who confess that simila-"rity, will it be acknowledged that the same "general maxims will apply, both to effects "mechanically produced, and those which "depend upon will and choice." Again, you say, p. 22, "To a principle of thought con-"ceived to be material, a change of circum-"stances may be essential to a difference of "volition; but when the mind is considered "as being in its own nature immaterial, and "therefore not subject to the laws of matter, "but as endued with a self-determining pow-"er, a variety of volition or determination "in the same situation or circumstances may "be admitted as possible, without any contra-"diction, or seeming difficulty at all."

Now

Now I really cannot conceive that the contradiction is at all the less glaring, or the difficulty more surmountable, on the hypothesis of the mind being immaterial. It does, indeed, follow that the mind, being immaterial, is not subject to the laws of matter; but it does not, therefore, follow that it is subject to *no laws at all,* and consequently has a self-determining power, independent of all laws, or rule of its determinations. In fact, there is the very same reason to conclude that the mind is subject to laws as the body. *Perception, judgment,* and the *passions,* you allow to be so, why then should the *will* be exempt from all law? Do not perception, judgment, and the passions, belong to the mind, just as much as the will; yet, notwithstanding this, it is only in certain cases that the powers of perception, judgment, or the passions, can be exerted. Admitting the mind, therefore, to be immaterial, it may only be in certain cases that a determination of the will can take place. You must find some other substance to which the will is to be ascribed, entirely different from that

that in which perception and judgment inhere, before you can conclude that its affections and acts are not invariable, and even neceſſary.

Beſides, according to all *appearances*, from which alone we can be authorized to conclude any thing, the deciſions of the will as invariably follow the diſpoſition of mind, and the motives, as the perception follows the preſentation of a proper object, or the judgment follows the perceived agreement or diſagreement of two ideas. This, at leaſt, is aſſerted by neceſſarians; and it does not depend upon the mind being material or immaterial whether the obſervation be juſt or not. If it be invalidated, it muſt be on ſome other ground than this. I am willing, however, to follow you through all that you alledge in ſupport of this argument.

"Moral neceſſity," you ſay, p. 45, "ariſes "from the influence of motives; which, as "they are not phyſical beings or ſubſtances, "cannot poſſibly act as one phyſical being "or "or substance does upon another." Again, p. 82, "where there is the greatest certainty, or necessity of a moral kind, there is always a possibility of a different choice." And, p. 46, "In the strict philosophical sense, nothing can be necessary, which is not physically so, or which it would not be a contradiction to the nature of things to suppose not to be, or to be otherwise than it is. Now this kind of necessity we clearly perceive in the case of one body acting upon another, and giving motion to it. But do arguments and motives bear the same physical relation to the determinations of the mind?"

I own I am rather surprized at the confidence with which you urge this argument, when it is maintained, and insisted on by necessarians, that arguments and motives *do* bear as *strict* a relation (call it physical or moral, or by whatever name you please) to determinations of the mind, as any other causes in nature to their proper effects; because, according to manifest

manifest appearances, the determinations of the will do, in fact, as certainly follow the apprehension of arguments and motives, as any one thing is ever observed to follow another in the whole course of nature; and it is just as much a contradiction to suppose the contrary in the one case as in the other, that is, a contradiction to the known and observed laws of nature; so that they must have been otherwise than they are now established, if any thing else should follow in those cases. No other kind of contradiction would follow in any case.

You say, however, p. 43, "Physical neces-
"sity is a necessity arising out of the nature
"of things, and immediately depending upon
"it; so that while things remain to be what
"they are, it would be a contradiction to sup-
"pose, that the consequences flowing from
"this kind of necessity can be different from
"those which do actually result from it. To
"say that any thing is necessary, in this sense,
"is the same as saying that it is a natural
"impossibility

"impossibility for it not to be, or to be dif-
"ferent from what it is." And, p. 44, you
"say, "The fall of a stone is the necessary
"effect of that law of gravity which is im-
"pressed upon it."

Now I do maintain, and all appearances will justify me in it, that a determination of the mind according to motives is, using your own words, that which arises from the very nature of the mind, and immediately dependent upon it; so that the mind remaining what it is, and motives what they are, it would be a contradiction to suppose that they should be different from what they are in the same circumstances. The parallel between material and immaterial natures is here most strict, and the inference the very same in the one case as in the other. If the fall of a stone be the necessary effect of gravity impressed upon it, or upon *body*, in the very *same sense* (because for the very *same reason*) the determination of the will is the necessary effect of the laws impressed upon it, or upon *mind*. This conclusion is as much grounded on facts and appearances as the other.

Nay, beginning with *mind*, I might, according to your mode of reasoning, say first, that, according to all appearances, the mind is necessarily determined by motives, for every thing we see in human nature confirms it. Mind is, therefore, subject to fixed laws, but matter is a thing totally different from mind. It cannot, therefore (whatever appearances may be) resemble mind in this, or any other respect, and consequently must be free from all fixed laws whatever. Thus might your own arguments be retorted upon you, and bring you to an evident absurdity; but, in my opinion, not a greater absurdity, or more contrary to fact, than that the mind is free from all fixed laws, and endued with a power of self-determination.

I wish, however, you would explain in what sense it would be a *contradiction* for a stone

stone not to fall to the ground. It is only from the obfervation of the *fact* that we find it does tend to the ground. *A priori,* it would have been juft as probable that it might have tended to recede from the ground, and to rife upwards. Where alfo would be the contradiction, in any proper fenfe of the word, if acids did not unite with alkalies, or if water fhould take fire and burn, like fpirit of wine? No perfon, I prefume, is fufficiently acquainted with the nature of things, to pronounce, that there would be any thing that could be called a *contradiction* in refults the very oppofite of what we fee do take place.

That which approaches the neareft to a properly neceffary effect, is *the receding of bodies after impulfe,* which you alfo maintain. But, though you fay you *clearly perceive* this neceffity, even this is a cafe in which, I will take upon me to fay, you cannot *demonftrate* the confequence to be neceffary. For, as I prefume I have fhewn at large, there is not *actual contact* in *all* cafes of feeming impulfe, and,

and, therefore, the receding of one body from another, in those circumstances, is owing to a real *repulsion*, which we can no more resolve into a *mechanical effect*, than we can those of *gravity*, because they both take place at a distance from the bodies concerned.

Now, as it is simply in consequence of the observed *uniformity of the fact*, that I conclude a stone will fall to the ground, it is equally in consequence of the observed uniformity of the fact, that I conclude the determination of the mind will follow the motive. An inference from observation is surely as decisive in one case as in the other; and this is clearly independent of all consideration of the mind being material or immaterial.

SECTION III.

SECTION III.

Of Certainty and Necessity.

YOU seem sometimes willing to allow that the determination of the will may be *certain*, that is, a definite thing in definite circumstances, and yet you maintain that it is not *necessary*; so that the arguments in favour of liberty are not affected by the concession.

"The argument itself," you say, p. 74, "may be resolved into this short question; whether certainty implies necessity, or, whether that which is morally certain, is, therefore, physically necessary?" And, p. 23, "it is not the influence of motives, but their necessary influence, that is denied."

Now, this is a cafe that I had confidered fo fully in my late *Treatife*, in my *Correfpondence with Dr. Price*, and in my *Letters to Dr. Horfley and Mr. Berington*, that I did not think I fhould have heard any more of it; and yet it feems you have read part, at leaft, of what I have advanced on that fubject; for you fay, p. 40, "The beft reafon that I can
"collect from all that the Doctor has advan-
"ced on this fubject, in favour of fuch a phy-
"fical connection refpecting the operations of
"the mind, is the univerfality or certainty
"of the effects, that is, of the determination
"which takes place in any given circumftan-
"ces. But though it be allowed that any
"particular effect would ever fo certainly
"follow on a ftate of mind, and a fituation
"of external objects correfponding with it,
"this will not prove the effect to be necef-
"fary. A moral certainty, and a phyfical
"neceffity, or a neceffity arifing out of the
"nature of things, cannot but imply in them
"very different ideas; nor is the latter by
"any means the confequence of the former."

You

You have, indeed, been able to collect, which was not difficult, (for I had occasion to repeat it several times) that, in favour of the *necessary* determination of the mind according to motives, I have urged the *certainty* and *universality* of such a determination; but I wonder you should not likewise have observed, that, in farther support of this, I added, that *certainty or universality is the only possible ground of concluding, that there is a necessity in any case whatever*; and to this, which you have not so much as noticed, you ought principally to have replied.

Please, Sir, to reflect a moment, and tell me distinctly, why you believe that there is a necessity that a stone must fall to the ground? Can it be any thing else than its having been observed that it *constantly* and *universally* does so? If, therefore, the determination follows the motives as certainly as a stone falls to the ground, there must be the very same reason to conclude, that, whether we see *why* it is so or not (which, indeed, we do not in the case of the falling of the stone) there is a *necessity* for its doing so. The difference cannot be in the *reality*, but only in the *kind* of necessity. The necessity must be the same, or equally strict and absolute in both, let the *causes* of the necessity in the two be ever so different.

(As I have told Dr. Horsley, but which you seem not to have attended to, (see *Correspondence with Dr. Price*, p. 223,) " I will allow
" as much difference as you can between mo-
" ral and physical causes. Inanimate mat-
" ter, or *the pen* that I write with, is not ca-
" pable of being influenced by motives, nor
" is the hand that directs the pen, but the
" mind that directs both.) I think I distin-
" guish these things better by the terms vo-
" luntary and involuntary, but these are mere
" words, and I make no comparison between
" them, or between moral and physical causes,
" but in that very respect in which you your-
" self acknowledge that they agree, *i. e.* the
" certainty with which they produce their
" respective effects. And this is the proper
" foundation

" foundation of all the neceffity that I afcribe
" to human actions. My conclufion, that men
" could not, in any given cafe, act otherwife
" than they do, is not at all affected by the
" *terms* by which we diftinguifh the laws and
" caufes that refpect the mind from thofe
" which refpect the external world. That
" there are *any laws*, and that there are *any*
" *caufes*, to which the mind is fubject, is all
" that my argument requires. Give me the
" thing, and I will readily give you the name."

" If" (as I obferved to Mr. Berington, *Treatife on Neceffity*, p. 174,) " the mind
" be, in fact, conftantly determined by mo-
" tives, I defire you would fay candidly why
" you object to the mere term *neceffity*, by
" which nothing is ever meant but the *caufe*
" *of conftancy*. It is only becaufe I fee a ftone
" fall to the ground conftantly, that I in-
" fer it does fo neceffarily, or according to
" fome fixed law of nature. And, pleafe to
" fay, whether you think it could happen,
" that the mind fhould be conftantly deter-
" mined

"mined by motives, if there was not a fixed law of nature from which that conſtant determination reſults."

Theſe paſſages, I preſume, you have overlooked. You certainly have not noticed them, or given due attention to them.

You muſt give me leave to obſerve, on this ſubject of *moral certainty*, that you ſeem ſometimes to have deceived yourſelf, by an ambiguous uſe of that term. Becauſe we are apt to be deceived in our judgments concerning the ſentiments and conduct of men, ſo that the greateſt certainty we can attain to with reſpect to them is frequently imperfect, we diſtinguiſh it from *abſolute certainty*, by calling it *moral*, and then apply the ſame term to other things, calling that a *moral certainty*, which is only a great *probability*. Thus, in the doctrine of chances, if there be a thouſand to one in my favour, I ſay there is a moral certainty that I ſhall ſucceed. But it does not follow that, becauſe the term *moral certainty* has

has by this means come to mean the same thing with *a high degree of probability*, nothing relating to the *mind* can have any thing more than a moral certainty, that is, a *probability*, attending it. Many propositions relating to the mind are as absolutely certain as any relating to the body. That the will constantly and invariably decides according to motives, must not, therefore, be concluded to have nothing more than a moral certainty attending it, merely because it is a truth relating to the *mind*, or to *morals*. It may be as absolutely certain as any truth in natural philosophy. It is the evidence of the *fact* that should be considered, and not the mere nominal distinctions of things.

For the farther illustration of this subject, I hope to satisfy you, that even all that you describe as most horrid and frightful in the doctrine of *necessity*, follows as evidently from your doctrine of *certainty*, provided it be a *real* certainty, though not such as you would chuse to call a *physical* one; and, therefore, that it can

can be nothing more than the mere *name* that you object to.

We will suppose that a child of yours has committed an offence, to which his mind was *certainly*, though *not necessarily*, determined by motives. He was not made, we will say, in such a manner as that motives had a *necessary* effect upon his mind, and *physically* or *mechanically* determined his actions, but only that his mind would in all cases *determine itself*, according to the same motives. You hear of the offence, and prepare for instant correction, not, however, on the idea that punishment is justifiable whenever it will reform the offender, or prevent the offences of others; but simply on your own idea, of its having been in the power of the moral agent to act otherwise than he had done.

Your son, aware of your principles, says, dear father, you ought not to be angry with me, or punish me, when you knew that I could not help doing as I have done. You placed

placed the apples within my reach, and knew that my fondness for them was irresistible. No, you reply, that is not a just state of the case, you were not under any *necessity* to take them, you were only so constituted as that you *certainly* would take them. But, says your son, what am I the better for this freedom from necessity? I wish I had been *necessarily* determined, for then you would not punish me; whereas now that I only *certainly* determine myself, I find that I offend just as much, and you always correct me for it.

A man must be peculiarly constituted, if, upon this poor distinction, he could satisfy himself with punishing his son in the one case, and not in the other. The offence he clearly foresaw would take place: for by the hypothesis, it was acknowledged to be *certain*, arising from his disposition and motives; and yet merely because he will not term it *necessary*, he thinks him a proper object of punishment. Besides, please to consider whether, if the child never *did* refrain from the offence

in

in those circumstances, there be any reason to think that he properly *could* have refrained. We judge of all *powers* only by their *effects*, and in all philosophy we conclude, that if any thing never *has* happened, and never *will* happen, there is a sufficient cause, though it may be unknown to us, why it never *could* happen. This is our only ground of concluding concerning what is possible or impossible in any case.

SECTION IV.

Of the Argument for the Doctrine of Necessity, from the Consideration of Divine Prescience.

IF there be any proposition strictly *demonstrable*, it is, as it appears to me, that *a contingent event is no object of prescience*, or that a thing which, in its own nature, *may,*

or

or *may not* be, cannot be certainly known to be future; for then it might be certainly known to be what it confessedly *may not be.* If, therefore, the mind of man be so constituted, as that any particular determination of his will may or may not take place, notwithstanding his previous circumstances, the Divine Being himself cannot tell whether that determination will take place or not. The thing itself is not subject to his controul, nor can be the object of his fore-knowledge.

To say, as you quote from some other person, p. 33, but without any declared approbation, that "fore-knowledge, if it does im-
"ply *certainty,* does yet by no means imply
"*necessity,* and that no other certainty is im-
"plied in it than such a certainty as would
"be equally in the things, though there was
"no fore-knowledge of them," is too trifling to deserve the least attention. You, therefore, in fact, give it up, and as, according to your system, the Divine Being cannot have this fore-knowledge, you take a good deal of
pains

pains to shew that he may do very well without it.

"Prescience," you say, p. 31, "is by no
"means essential to the government of free
"beings,———and a government of this na-
"ture, though prescience should be deemed
"inadmissible, as a contrariety to contin-
"gency in the event, may, notwithstand-
"ing, be as complete in its designs and ope-
"rations, as the utmost possible extent of
"knowledge, that is, the most perfect know-
"ledge united with almighty power, can
"make it." This, however, in these circumstances, may be very incomplete, and inadequate for its purpose. You add, p. 30,
"it cannot be impossible to almighty power,
"when the characters of men are known,
"because really existing, to bring about by
"means, which, previous to their operation,
"we cannot foresee, those events which he
"judges fit, and proper, for the maintainence
"and promotion of the well-being of his
"rational creation. And, after all, whatever

present

" present irregularities may be permitted to
" take place in the allotments of Providence
" to the sons of men, the grand and ultimate
" part of the plan of God's moral govern-
" ment, in the exact and equal distribution
" of rewards and punishments in a future
" scene of existence,—stands on the same
" firm and immovable grounds, whether
" the contingent actions of men be foreseen
" or not."

This, and what you farther advance on the same subject, I really am not able to read without pain and concern. You say, p. 32, that " the prophecies of scriptures do im-
" ply divine prescience in certain instances
" must be allowed." Now, unable as you evidently are to defend the very *possibility* of this prescience; this concession is rather extraordinary. To be truly consistent, and, at the same time, a believer in revelation, you ought to assert, how embarrassed soever you might be in making out the proof of it, that
there

there is no real fore-knowledge where a direct interference is not to be understood.

To lessen this difficulty, you say, p. 27, that, " by denying that prescience to God, " which is inconsistent with the idea of li" berty or agency in man, we only deny that " to belong to the supreme mind, which is, " in truth, no perfection at all. For, if it be " really impossible that even infinite know" ledge should extend to actions or events in " their own nature contingent, that is, where " proper liberty or agency is supposed, we no " more derogate from the perfection of the di" vine knowledge, by maintaining that God " cannot know such actions or events, than we " diminish his power by asserting that it can" not work contradictions, or what is really " no object of power at all. Equally must " it consist with the omniscience of the di" vine being, to say he cannot know that " which is impossible to be known, as it " does with his omnipotence to assert that
he

" he cannot do that which is impossible to
" be done."

I should think, however, that it must be a matter of deep regret to the human race, that the object of our supreme veneration and worship, on whom we constantly depend for *life, breath, and all things,* should want such an attribute as that of *prescience,* though it should be impossible that he could be possessed of it. It would certainly be more satisfactory to us to be dependent upon a being who had planned, and provided for the whole course of our existence, before we came into being, than on one who could not tell what turn things would take with respect to us the next moment of our lives, and who must, therefore, either interpose by a proper miracle when we fall into any unforeseen misfortune, or leave us to struggle with it, and be overwhelmed by it.

It is certainly no reflection upon me that I cannot see into the table I write on, and
discover

discover the internal texture of it; but I know that, as a philosopher, it would be a great perfection and advantage to me if I occasionally could.——I cannot help thinking that, with less ingenuity than you have employed to shew how the Divine Being might do without prescience, that is, without *omniscience*, you might prove that a power much short of *omnipotence*, and a degree of goodness much less than infinite, might suffice for him; and you might say it would be no reflection upon him at all to be less the object of love and reverence than we now conceive him to be. It can be no *detraction*, you might say, from any being, or *degradation*, to deny him what he never could have.

I rejoice that my opinions, whether true or false, oblige me to think with more reverence of the Supreme Being. It gives me a higher idea of my own dignity and importance, from a sense of my relation to him, and dependance upon him. You say, however, p. 216, that " the only character which the necessarian

"rian tenet, if confidered in its due extent,
"will admit of, as belonging to the uncreated
"mind, is a mixed one, in which, if I may fo
"fpeak, matchlefs virtues and matchlefs vices
"are blended together." And again, p. 188,
"he cannot but appear to be (horrid thought)
"the moft finful of all beings." *Horrid thought* indeed. But remember, it is not the neceffarian who has himfelf this idea of the object of his worfhip. This is only what *you* think for him; whereas it is yourfelf that deprive the Divine Being of his prefcience; which makes no fmall difference in the cafe. It is of little confequence to me what *you* think of the God that I worfhip, though it hurts me to hear him reproached in this manner. It is as little to you what *I* think of him whom you, or any other perfon, profeffes to worfhip; but what *we ourfelves* think of him is a very ferious bufinefs.

Being aware of the impoffibility of carrying on a fcheme of perfect moral government on your principles, without having recourfe to to a future state, you, however, make yourself easy about any irregularities that cannot be remedied here, on the idea that every thing that unavoidably goes wrong in this life, will be set to rights in another. But will not the same irregularities unavoidably arise from the same cause, the same self-determining power, in a future life as well as in this? You will hardly suppose that men will ever be deprived of a privilege which, in your estimation, is of so much importance to them. The nature of *man* will not be fundamentally changed, nor the nature of his *will*; and if this faculty retain the same character, it must be as much as ever perfectly uncontrolled either by the influence of motives, or by the deity himself. It will still, then, for reasons of its own, or for no reason at all, pay just as much or as little regard to every thing *foreign to itself*, as it pleases. Even *habits*, which may be acquired in this life, operate only as motives, or biases, inclining the mind to this or that choice, and nothing coming under that description has any decisive influence.

Here

Here is, therefore, from the unalterable nature of things, an everlasting source of irregularity, which must always be suffered for the present, and which can only be remedied in some future state. Thus periods of *disorder*, and periods of *rectification*, must succeed one another to all eternity. What a prospect does this view of things place before us!

You ask me, p. 33, " how far it would be
" agreeable to my ideas of civility and can-
" dour, had any writer on the side of liberty,
" under the warm impressions of an honest
" zeal against the manifest tendency of my
" *Illustrations of Philosophical Necessity*, adopted
" the same satirical strain that I myself, in a
" quotation you make from my treatise, used
" with respect to Dr. Beattie," and then you proceed to parody my own words, inserting my entire paragraph in a note.

" Thus," you say, p. 34, " our author, in
" the blind rage of disputation, hesitates not

"to deprive the ever-bleſſed God of the
"poſſibility of creating, what in revelation
"is repreſented as the nobleſt of his works,
"a being formed in his own likeneſs, that is
"*intelligent*, and *free*; ſubverting that great
"principle of liberty, than which nothing
"can be more eſſential to every juſt idea
"of a moral government; which yet we are
"every where throughout the books of ſcrip-
"ture taught, that the deity conſtantly ex-
"erciſes over mankind. This he has done
"rather than relinquiſh his fond attach-
"ment to the doctrines of materialiſm and
"neceſſity; doctrines which ſeem to draw
"after them an univerſal fataliſm, through
"the whole extent of nature, and which, if
"really true, it muſt be unſpeakably injurious
"both to the virtue and happineſs of the ge-
"nerality of mankind to make public."

I thank you, Sir, for the opportunity you have given me of trying how I ſhould feel on this occaſion. For, otherwiſe, we are ſo apt to overlook beams in our own eyes, while we can

can discover motes in the eyes of others, that I might not have attended to it; and I will tell you frankly how it is with me. Had I thought the reflection *just*, I should have felt it; though seeing it to proceed from an *honest zeal*, should not have thought it contrary to any thing that ought to be termed *civility*, or *candour*. But because I consider it as altogether founded on a mistake, I think it injurious to me, and unworthy of you.

I really suspect that neither you nor Dr. Beattie have sufficiently *attended to* the proofs of the divine prescience, either from reason or revelation. For they appear to me really stronger, and more strictly conclusive, than the arguments we have for his omnipotence or his infinite goodness; and the Divine Being himself proposes this as the very test and touchstone of *divinity itself*, so that a being not possessed of it is not, in a strict and proper sense, intitled to the appellation of *God*.— "Thus saith the Lord," Isa. xli. 22, concerning idols, "Let them shew us what shall
"happen

"happen. Let them shew the former things
"what they be, or declare us things to come.
"Let them shew the things that are to
"come hereafter, that we may know that they
"are Gods."

This, I own, is *preaching* to one whose office it is to preach to others; but I must preach on, and observe, that if you will only attend to the amazing variety and extent of the scripture prophecies, comprizing the fate of all the great empires in the world, the very *minutiæ* of the Jewish history, and all that is to befall the christian church to the very end of the world, you cannot entertain a doubt, but that every thought in the mind of every man (astonishing as the idea is) *must* have been distinctly perceived by the supreme ruler of all things from the beginning of the world.

You say, "the prophecies of scripture im-
"ply prescience *in certain instances*." This is greatly narrowing the matter, and giving an idea of it far below the truth. They not only

DOCTRINE OF NECESSITY. 43

only *imply*, but directly *assert* it in *numberless instances*; and it is implied, I may say, in an infinity of instances. Consider only, for I think it very possible that you may never have attended to it at all (as your principles will naturally incline you to look another way) consider, I say, how many millions of human volitions must have taken place from the beginning of the world, that really (directly or indirectly) contributed to the *death of Christ*, in the *very peculiar circumstances* in which it was actually foretold; volitions which, according to all appearance (from which alone we are authorized to form any conclusion) were perfectly natural, and uncontrolled by supernatural influence; and you cannot think it extravagant to say, that all the volitions of the minds of all men must have been known to him that could foretel that one event, *in its proper circumstances*. Not only must he have foreseen the tempers and dispositions of the rulers and common people of the Jews, the peculiar character of Pilate, Herod, and of every man immediately concerned in the

transtranfaction, and the peculiar manners and cuftoms of the Romans, but all that had *preceded*, to give the Romans their power, and form their manners and cuftoms, as well as thofe of the Jews and other nations. Think but a few minutes on the fubject, and it will fwell far beyond your power of conception, and overwhelm you with conviction. It impreffes my mind in fuch a manner, that, I own, I cannot help being extremely fhocked at the feeming *levity* with which you treat this moft ferious of all fubjects.

Such is the evidence of the divine prefcience from the confideration of the fcripture prophecies, that, if they be duly confidered, I do not think it in the power of the human mind to refift it; and without regard to any *confequences*, that metaphyfical fyftem which implies it, and is implied by it, *muft be true:* And when the whole fcheme is feen in its true colour and form, nothing can appear more admirable and glorious, more honourable to God, or more happy for man. But I will not enlarge

enlarge on the subject, though I can hardly forbear doing it.

Compared with this, how exceedingly low and poor must be their idea of the moral government of God, who hold him to have no fore-knowledge of the actions of men; and with what little satisfaction can they contemplate it? Only consider on that hypothesis, the millions, and millions of millions of volitions that take place every moment, on the face of this earth only, which the Divine Being, having no proper foresight of, cannot possibly control. For the mind of man is held to be as absolute, and uncontrolled, within its proper sphere, as the Divine Being is in his. The unknown effects of all these volitions he must always be anxiously watching, in order to remedy the inconveniencies that may arise from them as soon as possible; and he must have a distinct expedient provided for every contingency. What regularity or harmony can there be on such a scheme as this? What strange uncertainty, confusion, and

and perplexity, muſt reign every where! I am unable to proceed any farther with the ſhocking picture. I thank God that ſuch is not my idea of the government under which I really live.

To give our common readers an opportunity of judging of the paragraph which you think ſo obnoxious, and which you have taken care to bring into their view more than once, I ſhall myſelf recite the whole, with ſome things that precede and follow it.

"Among other things, our author gently touches upon the objection to the contingency of human actions from the doctrine of the divine preſcience. In anſwer to which, or rather in deſcanting upon which (thinking, I ſuppoſe, to chuſe the leſs of two evils) he ſeems to make no great difficulty of rejecting that moſt eſſential prerogative of the divine nature, though nothing can be more fully aſcertained by independent evidence from revelation, rather than give

" give up his darling hypothesis of human
" liberty; satisfying himself with observing,
" that *it implies no reflection on the divine power
" that it cannot perform impossibilities*. In the
" very same manner he might make himself
" perfectly easy if his hypothesis should com-
" pel him to deny any other of the attributes
" of God, or even his very being; for what
" reflection is it upon any person, or thing,
" that things impossible cannot be? Thus
" our author, in the blind rage of disputa-
" tion, hesitates not to deprive the ever-blessed
" God of that very attribute, by which, in
" the books of scripture, he expresly distin-
" guishes himself from all false Gods, and
" than which nothing can be more essentially
" necessary to the government of the universe,
" rather than relinquish his fond claim to the
" fancied privilege of *self-determination*; a
" claim which appears to me to be just as
" absurd as that of *self-existence*, and which
" could not possibly do him any good if he
" had it.

" Terrified,

"Terrified, however, as I am willing to suppose (though he does not express any such thing) at this consequence of his system, he thinks, with those who maintain a *trinity* of persons in the unity of the divine essence, and with those who assert the doctrine of *transubstantiation*, to shelter himself in the obscurity of his subject; saying, that *we cannot comprehend the manner in which the Divine Being operates.* But this refuge is equally untenable in all the cases, because the things themselves are, in their own nature, impossible, and imply a contradiction. I might just as well say that, though to us, whose understandings are so limited, *two* and *two* appear to make no more than *four*, yet in the divine mind, the comprehension of which is infinite, into which, however, we cannot look, and concerning which it is impossible, and even dangerous, to form conjectures, they may make *five*."

"Were

" Were I poffeffed of Dr. Beattie's talent
" of declamation, and had as little fcruple to
" make ufe of it, what might I not fay of
" the abfurdity of this way of talking, and
" of the horrible immoral confequences of
" denying the fore-knowledge of God? I
" fhould foon make our author, and all his
" adherents, as black as Atheifts. The very
" admiffion of fo untractable a principle as
" *contingency* into the univerfe, would be no
" better than admitting the Manichæan doc-
" trine of *an independent evil principle*. Nay,
" it would be really of worfe confequence,
" for the one might be controlled, but the
" other could not. But, I thank God, my
" principles are more generous, and I am as
" far from afcribing to Dr. Beattie all the
" real confequences of his doctrine (which,
" if he could fee with my eyes, he would
" reprobate as heartily as I do myfelf) as I
" am from admitting his injurious imputati-
" ons with refpect to mine."

I do assure you, Sir, I see nothing to retract in all this, though it is in the first of my works in which I mentioned the subject of *Necessity*; and I do not at all envy you the discovery, that, for the purposes of the moral government of God, *fore-knowledge* is a superfluous attribute.

SECTION V.

Of the Moral Tendency *of the Doctrine of Necessity.*

IT is on the subject of the *moral tendency* of the doctrine of necessity, that you imagine your arguments the strongest, and that you declaim with the greatest warmth and confidence. To all this, however, I think it unnecessary for me to reply. For, notwithstanding all you have written on this favourite

vourite theme, I am perfectly satisfied with what I have already advanced, and think it altogether unaffected by your reply. Besides, it behoves you, in the first place, to prove the doctrine to be false. For if it be true, the consequences will follow, and you as well as myself, must make the best we can of them. And I beseech you, for your own sake, that you would not represent them as so very frightful, lest, after all, *they should prove true.*

In the mean time, have some little tenderness for *me*, and consider with what sentiments, one who firmly believes the doctrine of necessity to be true, and at the same time to abound with the most glorious consequences, who imagines he feels it favourable to true elevation of mind, leading, in an eminent manner, to piety, benevolence, and self-government, must peruse the account you have been pleased to draw of his principles. The following are but a few of the features:

" I can-

"I cannot but think," you say, p. 242, "that the doctrine of necessity looks very much like a refinement on the old Manichæan notion of two independent principles of good and evil, which, in this system, are blended in one." "I cannot but think," you say, p. 183, "such sentiments as dangerous in their tendency, as they are false and absurd in themselves. They seem very materially, though undesignedly, to affect the moral character of the deity, and to be big with consequences the most fatal to the virtue and happiness of mankind. I cannot but look upon the promulgation of the scheme of necessity," p. 175, "as highly exceptionable, because it is likely to do unspeakable mischief. In the most exceptionable and dangerous principles of Calvinism, p. 238, the doctrine of necessity, when examined to the bottom, is really the very same." And in your preface, p. 4, you say, "nor can I help expressing very strong apprehensions of the dangerous tendency of the necessarian "tenet

"tenet as a practical principle; for that the generality of mankind would think themselves fully warranted in concluding that they could not, on any account, deserve punishment, and had therefore nothing to fear."

Before you had concluded, as you have done, that the publication of the doctrine of necessity *must* do such unspeakable mischief to *the generality of mankind,* you would have done well, I think, to have considered the state of the *fact.* Cast your eye over those of your acquaintance, and whom you know to be necessarians, especially those who have been so in early life, and who are the most attached to the doctrine. They are numerous enough to enable you to form some judgment of the practical tendency of their principles. Are their minds more depraved, their objects of pursuit less noble, or their exertions less strenuous, than you have reason to think they would have been if they had not been necessarians?

Had

Had I not been engaged in this controversy, you would probably have thought my own evidence as unexceptionable as that of any other person. But on this I lay no stress, though the compliments you pay me would give me some advantage in this case. If you say that *principles in general* have but an inconsiderable influence on practice, why should you suffer your fears to get the better of your reason in this particular case, and why should you urge what is, in fact, no proper argument at all, with more force, than every other consideration, respecting the real merits of the question?

However, light as I should be disposed to make of your accusation, I shall now treat it with the gravity that yourself will think it intitled to; and I think I may undertake to satisfy you, from your own mode of arguing, that there is no evil whatever to be apprehended from the doctrine of necessity, but, on the contrary, the greatest good, and that you evidently argue on principles inconsistent with each other when you throw so much odium on the scheme.

In

In the firſt place, you ſay, p. 149, that "on the ſcheme of neceſſity all is reſolved into a divine conſtitution, which is unalterably fixed. If any, therefore, are to ſucceed better, or be happier, in any part of their exiſtence than others, their ſuperior proſperity and happineſs will be infallibly ſecured to them; and though there is a certain diſpoſition of mind, and courſe of action, which are inſeparably connected with their ſucceſs and happineſs, as means to bring about thoſe events, yet the means as well as the end are alike neceſſary; and having no power to make either the one or the other at all different from what they are, or are to be, their lot, through the whole of their being, is by them abſolutely unalterable. What, again, I ſay, can have a ſtronger tendency to relax the mind, and ſink it into a ſtate of indolence and inactivity?"

Here then you reduce the neceſſarian to a ſtate of abſolute *inactivity*, that is, indiſpoſed to to *any purfuits*, virtuous or vicious. For your argument, if it goes to any thing, goes to both alike.

But, on the other hand, you conftantly fuppofe, fo that I have no occafion to quote particular paffages, that the neceffarian will, of courfe, give himfelf up to the gratification of all his paffions, and purfue without reftraint whatever he apprehends to be his intereft or happinefs.

Here then, notwithftanding the natural *indolence* of the neceffarian, you are able, when your argument requires it, to find a confiderable fource of *activity* in him; becaufe you have difcovered, that, like other men, he has *paffions*, and a *regard to his intereft and happinefs*.

But, furely, it is not difficult to conceive, that this activity, from whatever fource it arifes, may take a good as well as a bad turn, and lead to virtue or vice, according as it is directed.

directed. If the gratification of our lower appetites leads to evil, the gratification of the higher ones, as benevolence, &c. (of which, I hope, you will admit that a necefsarian, being a man in other respects, may be possessed) must lead to good; and that, if false notions of interest and happiness instigate a man to vice, just notions of his interest and happiness must lead to virtue. In fact, therefore, upon your own principles, nothing is requisite to convert even a necefsarian from vice to virtue, but the better informing his understanding and judgment, which you expressly allow to be mechanical things, being always determined by a view of the objects presented to them, and to have nothing of self-determination belonging to them.

This, if there be any force in your own reasoning, must be a sufficient answer to every thing that you so pathetically and repeatedly urge concerning the mischiefs to be dreaded from the doctrine of necessity. It would

would be very disagreeable to me to go over all that you say on this subject, and, therefore, I am glad to find that I have no occasion to do it.

I am sorry to find that, in pursuing your supposed advantage so inconsiderately as you do, you, in fact, plead the cause of vice, and represent it as triumphing over every consideration drawn from the present or a future state. "How is a vicious man," you say, p. 185, "who finds that the present "natural good of pleasure or profit results "from the gratification of his appetites, "and from defrauding or over-reaching his "neighbour, to be persuaded to think that "vice is productive of evil to him here? On "the supposition that there is no moral dif- "ference in things, all moral arguments "against the course of conduct to which his "appetites or inclinations prompt him, im- "mediately vanish. As long, therefore, as "he can make his present conduct consistent "with what is his natural good, or which
"he

"he looks upon to be so, that is, with sensi-
tive pleasure, or his worldly advantage, all
is right and well, so far as regards the present scene of things."

Now I am really surprized that you, who have been so long a preacher, could not, on this occasion, recollect any thing in answer to such a libertine as this, without having recourse to arguments drawn from a future state, and even independent of moral considerations, of which it is but too apparent that mere sensualists and worldly-minded persons make little account. Do no evils arise to the bodily constitution, to the mental faculties, or to society, from habitual excess in eating or drinking, or from the irregular indulgence of other natural appetites? And short of excess we are within the bounds of virtue; for in fact, nothing is ever properly termed excess, but what does terminate (and it is so called because it terminates) in pain and misery. Is it not possible that a man may both shorten his life, and make his short life miserable, by his vices? Only reperuse your own excellent sermon, intitled, *The insanity of the Sensualist*, written long before this controversy; and you will find many valuable observations to this purpose.

Supposing conscience entirely out of the question, are injustice and oppression always successful, and are there not many proverbs founded on general experience, teaching even the vulgar, in a variety of expression, that, some how or other, ill-gotten wealth does not contribute to happiness? Or, exclusive of the natural course of things, are there no such things as laws and magistrates in human society? Are there no gallows, gibbets, or wheels, to which flagrant wickedness may bring a man? Now may not a necessarian see the necessary connection of these *natural evils* with a course of vicious indulgence, as well as any other person; and, fully apprehending this, can he pursue the one without chusing his own destruction, of which I fancy you will allow that he is just as incapable as any person whatever. Besides,

Besides, it is very unfair to say that because a necessarian considers those things which are generally termed *moral*, as coming ultimately under the same description with things *natural*, that, therefore, he believes there are no such things at all. You well know that he does not consider these things as at all the less *real*, though, as a philosopher, he chuses to give them another name. A sense of right and wrong, the stings of conscience, &c. (which, however, will not, in general, be so much felt by those who believe no future state) are things that actually exist, by whatever names they be signified, and will be felt in a greater or less degree by the most hardened transgressor.

Dr. Hartley and myself have endeavoured to shew that the peculiar feeling of *remorse*, arising from ascribing our actions to ourselves, can never vanish, or cease to influence us, till we arrive at such a comprehension of mind, as will enable us habitually to ascribe every thing to God, and that when

we

we are arrived at this state, we shall live in communion with God, and shall stand in no need of such a motive to virtue. Before this period, let a man be speculatively a necessarian, or whatever he will, and let him pretend what he pleases, it will be *naturally impossible* for him not to feel all the pungency of remorse, whenever even yourself would say that he ought to feel it. You must invalidate our reasoning on this subject, from the consideration of the nature of the human mind, before you can make it appear that a necessarian, *as such*, will be a bad man. But as you lay so very much stress on this subject of remorse of conscience, I will discuss the matter a little farther with you.

You say that remorse of conscience implies that a man thinks he could have acted otherwise than he did. I have no objection to admit this, at the same time, that I say he deceives himself in that supposition. I believe, however, there are few persons, even those who blame themselves with the greateft

est pungency, but, if they will reflect, will acknowledge, that in so supposing, they leave out the consideration of the situation they were in at the time of the transaction, and that with the same disposition of mind that they had then, and the same motives, they should certainly have acted the same part over again; but that having, since that time, acquired a different disposition, and different views of things, they unawares carry them back, and consider how they would have acted with their present acquired dispositions. However, their disposition being really altered by what has occurred to them since, they would not *now* act the same part over again, and therefore, all the proper ends of remorse are sufficiently answered.

If you say that the peculiar feeling of remorse is founded on a mistake, I answer, so are the peculiar feelings of anger in most cases, and likewise the peculiar feelings of all our passions, and that a philosopher, who should have strength of mind to consider his situation,

situation, would do the same things coolly and effectually without that *stimulus,* that the vulgar do with it. He would punish an offender without anger, and he would reform his own conduct without remorse. But neither you nor myself, necessarian as I am, can pretend to this degree of perfection. It is acquired by experience; and the firmest belief of the doctrine of necessity can only accelerate our progress towards it to a certain degree. All this I have endeavoured to explain in my *Additional Illustrations,* but you have not noticed it.

What you say of the little influence of the motives to virtue which the necessarian can draw from the consideration of a *future life,* by no means concerns the necessarian as such. " In relation to futurity," you say, p. 185, " it is naturally to be supposed, that a man " of this disposition" (*i. e.* a vicious necessarian) " will not concern himself about it, or " if he does, his necessarian principle, by " holding up to his view his future moral
" good

"good or happiness, as secured to him by
"his omnipotent Creator, will lead him ha-
"stily to pass over all intermediate sufferings
"with which he is threatened, how long or
"severe soever, considering them only as na-
"tural evils, which he can no more avoid
"than the course of action which is connected
"with them."

You know very well that they are not necessarians only who believe, that all the sufferings of a future life are corrective, and will terminate in the reformation of those who are exposed to them. And a man must not be a necessarian, but the reverse of one, and the reverse of every thing that *man* is, before he can be made to slight the consideration either of present or future evils, especially long and severe ones, provided he really believes them, and gives proper attention to them. But with this *belief* and *attention* they cannot but influence any man who regards his own happiness, and who believes the inseparable connection between virtue

and

and happiness (which no man believes more firmly than the necessarian) to have recourse to a life of virtue, as the only road to happiness, here or hereafter. And having, from whatever motive, begun to tread this path, he will persist in it from a variety of other and better principles.

That you should prefer the Calvinistic doctrine of *eternal punishments*, horrible as you say it is, to that of *universal restoration to virtue and happiness*, could surely be dictated by nothing but your abhorrence of the doctrine of necessity in general, to which it is usually, but not necessarily, an appendage. "I cannot but be of opinion," you say, p. 239, "that the persuasion of the final "restoration of all the wicked to virtue and "happiness, which it" (the doctrine of necessity) "supports, will, in its natural ope- "ration, have a very pernicious influence on "the unsettled minds of the generality of "mankind: while the doctrine of eternal re- "medilefs torments for the non-elect, taught

"by

DOCTRINE OF NECESSITY.

" by Calvinism, horrible as it is in itself,
" may, in the way of restraint, have a con-
" siderable effect, and in some instances may
" probably produce an external reformation
" of life."

You may just as well say, that a civil magistrate who punishes without reason, mercy, or bounds, will be more respected than an equitable judge, who exacts an adequate punishment for every offence. Besides, the doctrine of eternal punishments for the offences of a short life is so very absurd, that it must ever be attended with a secret incredulity. At least, a man, though wicked, yet thinking he does not deserve the everlasting pains of hell, will not believe that he shall be sent thither, and therefore will indulge a notion that he shall go to heaven, and escape punishment altogether. But I need not argue this point, as it does not belong to me as a necessarian to do it. I have already argued in my *Institutes of natural and revealed Religion.*

SECTION VI.

What makes Actions a Man's own, *and* depending on himself.

TO what I have already advanced in reply to your remarks on the moral influence of the doctrine of necessity, and the comparison of it with the Calvinistic doctrine of predestination, I shall add, in a separate section, some considerations on men's actions as *depending on themselves,* and being *their own,* on which you lay so much stress, and which runs through your whole book. Now I am confident that, in what you say on this subject, you deceive yourself by the use of words, or you could not draw the consequences that you do from what you suppose to be my doctrine on this subject.

Strictly

Strictly and philosophically speaking, my success in any thing I wish to accomplish, depends upon myself, if my own exertions and actions are necessary links in that chain of events by which alone it can be brought about. And, certainly, if I do know this, and the object or end be desirable to me, this desire (if it be of sufficient strength) cannot but produce the exertion that is necessary to gain my end. This reasoning appears to me extremely easy, and perfectly conclusive, and yet, though I have repeated it several times, and have placed it in a variety of lights, you do not seem to have considered it. I shall, therefore, give another instance, and add some farther illustrations.

Can I have a sufficiently strong wish to answer your book, and not of course read it, mark proper extracts from it, arrange them, write my remarks upon them, then transcribe them for the press, and put them into the hands of a bookseller or printer, &c. when I know, that if all this be not done, the book will never be answered? Surely my firm belief that all these things are necessarily connected, must convince me of the necessity of setting about the work, if I wish to do it at all; and my *wish* to have it done is here to be supposed, as having arisen from a variety of previous circumstances.

If, therefore, I shall certainly find myself disposed to act just as I now do, believing my actions to be necessary, your objection to my doctrine on this account cannot have a sufficient foundation. You say, that if the thing *must be*, it *must be*; if your book *is to be* answered by me, it *will be* answered by me; and that I may, therefore, make myself easy about it, and do nothing. I answer, that so I should, either if I had no desire to have it done, which happens not to be the case, or if I thought that no exertions of mine were necessary to gain my end, which is not the case neither. On this consideration depends the capital distinction that I make between the

the doctrines of philosophical necessity and Calvinistic predestination.

The Calvinists make the work of conversion to be wholly of God's free and sovereign grace, independent of every thing in the person thus regenerated or renovated, and to which he cannot in the least contribute. In this work, they say, God is the sole agent, and men altogether passive; that both to *will* and to *do* is of God's pleasure; and so much so, that without his immediate agency, to which nothing on the part of man can contribute, let a man exert himself ever so much, in the use of all possible means, yet all his volitions and all his actions would be only sinful, and deserving of the wrath and curse of God to all eternity.

In this case I do not see what a man can have to do, because his doing, or his not doing, is equally unconnected with the end he has in view. But this is the very reverse of the doctrine of philosophical necessity, which supposes

supposes a necessary connection between our endeavours and our success; so that if only the *desire of success*, the first link in this chain, be sufficiently strong, all the rest will follow of course, and the end will be certainly accomplished.

According to the Calvinists, there may be the most earnest desire, without a man's being at all the nearer to his end, because the *desire* and the *end* have no necessary connection, by means of intermediate links, as we may say, in the chain that joins them.

It is on this ground that Dr. Hartley justly supposes that the doctrine of necessity has a tendency to make men exert themselves, which he makes the fifth advantage attending the scheme. "It has a tendency," he says, p. 344, of my edition, "to make us labour "more earnestly with ourselves and others, "particularly children, from the greater cer- "tainty attending all endeavours that operate "in a mechanical way."

Another

Another of your arguments relating to this subject, I really cannot treat with so much seriousness as you will probably expect. I shall not, however, dwell long upon it, and with this I shall close the section.

I had observed, that a volition may be termed *mine*, if it takes place in my mind. Animadverting on this, you say, p. 80, "Can that be truly said to be my volition, my act, which is produced by something over which I had no power. On that ground every thing that takes place in my body, as well as in my mind, may with equal propriety be called my act or volition;— and so the circulation of the blood, and the pulsation of the heart, may with equal reason be called my volitions."

Now, Sir, is not *judgment* always called an *act of the mind*, as well as volition? But has any man power over this? Is not this necessarily determined by the view of arguments, &c.? You will not deny it. Does it not,

not, therefore, follow, on your own principles, that whatever paffes in your body, as well as in your mind, may with equal propriety be called an act of your judgment;—and fo the circulation of your blood, and the pulfation of your heart, may with equal reafon be called your *judgment*. But the very fame things were before proved to be *volitions*. *Ergo, judgments* and *volitions* are the fame things. By the fame mode of reafoning, it would be eafy to prove your head to be your feet, and your feet your head, and both of them to be the fame with your underftanding, or any thing elfe belonging to you.

SECTION

SECTION VII.

Of the proper Object of this Controversy, and a summary View of the principal Sources of Mistake with respect to it.

AS I take it for granted you would not have engaged in this controversy, especially after a person for whom you profess so great an esteem as Dr. Price, without thinking you felt yourself fully equal to it, and without being determined to see it fairly out, I shall take the liberty, which I hope you will also do with respect to me, (that we may save ourselves as much trouble as possible) to point out what I think will be of use to us in conducting it. And in doing this, I shall purposely go over some of the ground I have already trod, but in a different direction,

direction, hoping that different views of the same objects may be both pleasing and useful.

In general, I think, we shall do well to consider things as much as possible *without the use of words*, at least such words as are, on either side, charged with being the causes of mistake. I shall treat of the principal of them separately.

1st. Of the Term AGENT.

IN the farther prosecution of this debate, do not begin, as you have done now, with assuming that man, in consequence of having a power of choice, is an *agent,* and that being an agent, he cannot be a mere passive being, acted upon by motives, &c. but must be possessed of a power of proper self-determination. In fact, this is no better than taking for granted the very thing in dispute, and therefore you might as well, with Dr. Beattie, disclaim all *reasoning* on the subject, and assert your liberty on the footing of *common sense,* or *instinct* only.

The

The only unexceptionable method is, to attend to the real *phenomena of human nature*, and to confider the known actions of men in known fituations, in order to determine whether our volitions, which precede all our actions, and direct them, be not always *definite in definite circumftances*. If you admit this, and I think it almoft impoffible not to admit it, you admit all that I contend for; becaufe it will then follow, that from a man's birth to his death, there is an unalterable chain of *fituations* and *volitions*, invariably depending on one another. Your faying that, if this be the cafe, man is no *agent*, will avail nothing; for if that word imply more than the actual phenomena will authorize, the agency of man, in that fenfe of the word, flattering as it may found, muft be given up.

Dr. Price does, in fact, allow that men's volitions are definite in definite circumftances, for he fays it is the greateft abfurdity to fuppofe that men ever act either without or againft motives, but that the felf-determining

ing power is wanted only when the motives are equal; which, considering how very seldom this can be supposed to be the case, reduces this boasted liberty of man, in my opinion, to a very small matter, hardly worth contending for.

In this you differ from him. For you carefully avoid making that concession, and always, at least generally, suppose the mind capable of acting contrary to any motive whatever. But then you will do well to consider whether, consistently with the phenomena, Dr. Price could avoid making that concession, alarming as you may think it; and whether it be probable that, in fact, men ever do act either without, or contrary to motives. And if he never *does*, you will not easily prove that he *can*.

If man be an agent, in your sense of the word, that is, if his will be properly *self-determined*, you must shew that nothing foreign to the will itself, nothing that can come under

under the description of *motive,* or the circumstances in which the mind is, regularly precedes the determination. For if any such foreign circumstances, any thing that is not *mere will,* does constantly precede every determination, we are certainly authorized, by the established rules of philosophizing, to consider these circumstances as the proper causes of the determination, and may, therefore, say that the will is influenced or acted upon by them, and so, going backwards in the same train, we shall conclude that there can be no more than one proper agent in the universe.

2. *Of Responsibility.*

LET us likewise consider the nature and use of *moral government,* as much as possible, without the use of such words as *responsibility, praise, blame,* &c. and only consider how a wise governor would treat beings whose wills should be invariably influenced by motives; and if the proper ends of government would,

in

in fact, be answered by annexing happiness to such actions as we call virtuous, and misery to such as we call vicious, (so that every thing we now see or expect would be done) it will follow, that, for any thing that appears to the contrary, we *may* be so constituted. If the word *responsibility*, as you arbitrarily define it, will not apply to such a system, it ought to be discarded from the language of philosophers.

Take the same course with the words *merit* and *demerit*, *virtue* and *vice*, &c. and on this subject, attend particularly to what Dr. Hartley, in a very short compass, most excellently observes. "It may be said," says he, p. 343, "that the denial of free will
" destroys the distinction between virtue and
" vice. I answer, that this is according as
" these words are defined. If free will be
" included in the definition of virtue, then
" there can be no virtue without free will.
" But if virtue be defined *obedience to the will*
" *of God, a course of action proceeding from the*
" *love*

" *love of God,* or *from benevolence,* &c. free
" will is not at all neceffary; fince thefe af-
" fections and actions may be brought about
" mechanically.

" A folution analogous to this may be
" given to the objection from the notions of
" merit and demerit. Let the words be de-
" fined, and they will either include free
" will, or, not including it, will not require
" it; fo that the propofition, *merit implies free*
" *will,* will either be identical or falfe."

In all that you have faid on the fubject of refponfibility, you take your own principles for granted, and then it can be no wonder that all your conclufions follow. You make it effential to refponfibility that man has a power, independent of his difpofition of mind at the particular time, and of all motives, of acting otherwife than he did, and you take not the leaft notice of what I have advanced on that fubject in the *Correfpondence with Dr. Price,* p. 150, &c. where I fhow that, notwithftanding

withstanding it be not in the power of moral agents to act otherwise than they do, yet that a moral governor, who consults the good of his subjects (whose minds and whose conduct he knows to be influenced by motives) must treat them in the very same manner that you yourself acknowledge he ought to do. He will apply suffering with propriety, and, with good effect in any case in which the apprehension of it will so impress the minds of his subjects, offenders and others, as to influence their wills to right conduct. So that, as I have observed, p. 151, " though the vulgar and philo-
" sophers may use different language, they
" will always see reason to act in the very
" same manner. The *governor* will rule vo-
" luntary agents by means of rewards and
" punishments; and the *governed*, being vo-
" luntary agents, will be influenced by the
" apprehension of them. It is consequently
" a matter of indifference in what language
" we describe actions and characters." This you should have particularly considered and have replied to. You must not tell me what
the

the word *responsibility* requires; but you must show that, supposing men to be what I suppose them, the supreme ruler ought to have treated them otherwise than he actually has done. If not, every fact exactly corresponds with my hypothesis, and then on what can your objection be founded, except on something that is merely verbal.

3. *Of the Prejudice arising from the terms* MACHINE *and* NECESSITY.

YOU mislead and deceive yourself, I am persuaded, not a little, by the frequent use of the opprobrious term *machine*, saying, in the first place that, because a man wills *necessarily*, that is, definitely in definite circumstances, he wills *mechanically*; and then having made a man into a *machine*, you, unknown to yourself, connect with it every thing opprobrious and degrading belonging to a common clock, or a fulling-mill.

But you might easily correct this by only considering what you yourself allow to be necessary relating to the mind of man, viz. *perception* and *judgment*. Is there not something inconceivably more excellent in these powers than in those of common machines, or mills, and even something that bears no resemblance to any thing belonging to them, though they all agree in this one circumstance, that their respective affections are necessary? Now suffer your mind to be sufficiently impressed with the wonderful nature and excellence of the powers of *perception* and *judgment*, and you cannot think the *will* at all degraded by being put on a level with them, even in the same respect in which they all agree with any common machine, or a mill, viz. that all its affections are definite in definite circumstances, though this property be best expressed by the term *necessary*.

If you suffer your mind to be affected by such prejudices as these, you may decline applying

applying the term *substance* to the mind, because it is likewise applied to wood and stone, and oblige yourself to invent some other term by which to distinguish it from them.

With respect to the Divine Being, you will not scruple to say, that his actions are always definite in definite circumstances, and if you decline applying the term *necessary* to them, it is only because you conceive that it implies something more than *definite in definite circumstances*, whereas the two phrases are perfectly synonymous, and it is nothing but the word that you can dislike. The *reasons* why we say that any affection or action is necessary, and why it is definite in definite circumstances, are the very same, and cannot be distinguished in the mind. It is the *constant observation of its taking place in those circumstances.*

It is because we see that a clock always strikes when the hands are in certain positions,

ons, that we conclude it always *will* do so, and, therefore, *necessarily must* do so, or that (whether it be known or unknown to us) there is a *cause* why it cannot be otherwise. Now, can you help applying this mode of reasoning, and, consequently, this phraseology, to the mind, and even the divine mind, and, at the same time, be free from weak and unworthy prejudices? (For, if the will cannot act but when motives are present to it, and if it always determines definitely in definite circumstances with respect to motives, you cannot but conclude that there is a sufficient reason, known or unknown to you, why it *must* be so, and you can have no reason to suppose that it ever can be otherwise.) And, in this case, whether you scruple to say, that such a determination can be called *action*, or be said to be *necessary*, your ideas of the things are the same. (If any thing always *will* be so, there can be no good reason why we should scruple to say that it *must*, and *must necessarily* be so.)

The

The Divine Being, you will allow, notwithstanding the incomprehensibility of his nature, always acts definitely in definite circumstances. It would be a weakness and imperfection to do otherwise. In fact, it is no more a degradation of him to say that he acts *necessarily*, than that his essence may be termed *substance*, or *being*, in common with that of the human mind, or even that of wood and stone.

You will say, and justly enough, that this observation applies to the Divine Being only as *actually existing*, and *operating*; and that originally, and before the creation, when there were no external circumstances by which his actions could be determined, his volitions must have been, in the proper and strict philosophical sense of the word, *free*. But then there never can have been a time, to which that observation applies, because there never can have been any time in which the Deity did not *exist*, and consequently *act*.

For, supposing him not to have been employed in creation, &c. (which, however, I think we can hardly avoid supposing) he must at least have *thought,* and *thinking,* you will not deny to be the acting of the mind. The origin of action, therefore, in your sense of the word, that is, the origin of self-determination, is the same as the origin of the Deity, concerning which we know nothing at all.

Besides, how can you, or any of Dr. Clark's admirers, think it any degradation to the Deity, that he should *act* necessarily, when you allow that he *exists* necessarily? Is not the term just as opprobrious in the one case as in the other? Nay, might it not rather be supposed, by analogy, that the actions of the being whose existence is necessary, must be necessary too. With respect to your notion of dignity and honour, I would ask, Is not the *existence* of any being or thing, of as much importance to him, as his *acting?* Is not

not then his being subject to necessity as great a reflection upon him in the former case as in the latter? In short, every thing that you consider as *degrading* and *vilifying* in man, on account of his being subject to necessity, in his existence or actions, might, if I were disposed to retort so trifling and mistaken a consideration, be applied to the Divine Being himself. What I now observe is only to take off the force of your prejudice against the doctrine of necessity, on account of its exhibiting man, as you suppose, in a degrading and unimportant light.

THE CONCLUSION.

Dear Sir,

I HAVE now gone over all the topicks that I think of much importance to discuss with you. I might have taken a much larger compass; but I was unwilling to take in more objects than such as I thought I might possibly throw some new light upon. As to what you say concerning the doctrine of the scriptures, and several other articles, I leave the field open to you, being fully satisfied with what I have already advanced, and having nothing material to add to it.

You will probably think there is an appearance of *arrogance* in the tone of this letter,

ter. But in this, I think, you will do me injuftice; my manner of writing being nothing more than what neceffarily arifes from the fullnefs of my perfuafion concerning the truth and importance of the doctrine I contend for; and this, I think, is not greater than your own. But in this I muft appeal to indifferent perfons, if any fuch there be, who will give themfelves the trouble to read what we have written.

We all fee *fome things* in fo clear and ftrong a light, that, without having any high opinion of our own underftandings, we think we may challenge all the world upon them. Such all perfons will think to be moft of the propofitions of Euclid, and fuch, I dare fay, with you are many tenets in theology. You would not hefitate, I prefume, to maintain that *bread and wine* cannot be *flefh and blood*, againft even a Boffuet, or a Thomas Aquinas, than whom, it is probable, the world never produced a greater man; and that *three perfons,*

fons, each poffeffed of all the attributes of God, muft make more in number than *one God,* againſt all the divines that the three churches of Rome, England, and Scotland, could name to hold the difputation with you. And, though it fhould be deemed, as by them it certainly would be, the height of arrogance in you to hold out this challenge, it would not give you any difturbance; nor, in fact, would you think very highly of yourfelf, though you fhould gain a decided victory in fuch a conteft.

Now, this happens to be my cafe with refpect to the doctrine of Neceffity. I really think it the cleareft of all queſtions, the truth of it being as indubitable as that the three angles of a right-lined triangle are equal to two right angles, or that *two* and *two* make *four,* and, therefore, I have no feeling either of *fear* or *arrogance,* in challenging the whole world in the defence of it. This argument I compare to fuch ground as one man may defend

defend against an army. It is, therefore, absolutely indifferent to me by *whom*, or by *how many*, I be assailed. You would, probably, say the same with respect to the doctrine of Liberty, at least the style in which your book is written seems to speak as much; and yet I by no means think you deficient in modesty, any more than I do in understanding and ability. I only wish, therefore, that, notwithstanding the confidence with which I have written, you would put the same candid construction on my conduct, that I do on yours.

I make allowance for our difference of opinion, on account of the different lights in which we happen to see things, or in which they have been represented to us; nor do I at all expect that any thing I have now advanced, or am capable of advancing, will make the least change in your view of things. A change in things of so much moment, which would draw after it a thousand other changes,

changes, is not to be expected either in you or myself, who are both of us turned forty, and who were, I suppose, metaphysicians before twenty. Judging of ourselves by other men, we must conclude that our present *general system of opinions*, whether right or wrong, is that which we shall carry to our graves. Those who are younger than we are, and whose principles are not yet formed, are alone capable of judging between us, and of forming their opinions accordingly; and in that respect, they may derive an advantage from these publications that we cannot derive from them ourselves.

We see every day such instances of *confirmed judgments* in things of the greatest, as well as of the least moment, as ought to make the most confident of us to pause, though every man is necessarily determined by his own view of the evidence that is before him. I am well aware that, let me place the evidence for the doctrine of necessity in the strongest

strongest and clearest light that I possibly can, arguing either from the nature of the will, observations on human life, or the consideration of the divine prescience; let me describe the doctrine of imaginary liberty as a thing ever so absurd, and impossible in itself, as totally foreign to, and inconsistent with all principles of just and moral government, and supplying no foundation whatever for praise or blame, reward or punishment; the generality of my readers will never get beyond the very threshold of the business. They will still say, "Are we not conscious of our freedom, cannot we do whatever we please; sit still, walk about, converse, or write, just as we are disposed?" and they will fancy that all my reasoning, plausible as it may seem, cannot, in fact, deserve any attention; and even though they should be silenced by it, they will not be the nearer to being convinced.

But just so we see it to be in politics. Let such writers as Dr. Price explain ever so clearly

clearly the injuftice of taxing any people without their confent, fhewing that the fame power that can compel the payment of one penny, may compel the payment of the laft penny they have, and that a foreign people or nation, eafing themfelves by laying the burthen upon others, will be difpofed to proceed as far as poffible in this way; ftill he will never fatisfy many perfons of landed property in this country, who will anfwer all he can fay by one fhort argument, the force of which they feel and comprehend, faying, "What, "fhall we pay taxes, and the Americans "none?" The Doctor may repeat his arguments, and exhibit them in every poffible light, he will get no fufficient attention to them from a perfon whofe whole mind is occupied with the *fingle idea*, of his paying taxes, and the Americans paying none.

Notwithftanding, therefore, all that I fhall ever be able to write in favour of the doctrine of neceffity, your fuppofed *confcioufnefs of liberty, ty*, and of if popular arguments (though often anathith they really make againſt your hypotheſis, will always ſecure you *nine* out of *ten* of the generality of our readers. All that I can do muſt be to make the moſt of my *tenth man*; and, if I poſſibly can, fancy his ſuffrage equivalent to that of your nine. And to allay your fears of another kind, be aſſured that this tenth man will generally be of ſo *quiet* and *ſpeculative* a turn, that you need be under no apprehenſion of his engaging in riots or rebellions. He will neither murder you in your bed, nor ſubvert the ſtate.

I think, therefore, now that I have advanced, I verily believe, all that I can, in ſupport of my opinion, I ought to acquieſce in the ſucceſs of my labours, be it more or leſs. I ſee nothing *new* in any thing that you have advanced, and you will ſee nothing new, at leaſt more forcible, in this reply. I do not, however, make any fixed reſolutions.

If you make a *rejoinder*, as I think you *ought*, and will be advised to do, I, true to my principles as a necessarian, *shall act as circumstances shall determine me.*)

I am, with much respect,

DEAR SIR,

Your's sincerely,

J. PRIESTLEY.

Calne, Aug. 1779.

CONTENTS.

SECT. I. *Of the Argument for the Doctrine of* NECESSITY *from the Consideration of the Nature of* CAUSE *and* EFFECT. - - - p. 6

SECT. II. *How far the* ARGUMENTS *for the Doctrine of* NECESSITY *are affected by the Consideration of the* SOUL *being material or immaterial.* p. 11

SECT. III. *Of* CERTAINTY *and* NECESSITY. p. 21

SECT. IV. *Of the* ARGUMENT *for the Doctrine of* NECESSITY, *from the Consideration of* DIVINE PRESCIENCE. - - - - p. 30

SECT. V. *Of the* MORAL TENDENCY *of the Doctrine of* NECESSITY. - - p. 50

SECT. VI. *What makes* ACTIONS *a* MAN'S OWN, *and* DEPENDING ON HIMSELF. p. 68

SECT. VII. *Of the proper* OBJECT *of this Controversy, and a summary View of the principal Sources of Mistake with respect to it.* p. 75

The CONCLUSION. - - p. 90

ERRATA.

Page 4, line 8, for *presented* read *present*.
P. 33 l. 14, for *scriptures* read *scripture*.

A CATALOGUE OF BOOKS,

WRITTEN BY
JOSEPH PRIESTLEY, LL.D. F.R.S.

AND PRINTED FOR
J. JOHNSON, Bookseller, at No. 72, St. Paul's Church-Yard, London.

1. THE History and Present State of Electricity, with original Experiments, illustrated with Copper-Plates, 4th Edition, corrected and enlarged, 4to. 1l. 1s. Another Edition 2 vols. 8vo. 12s.

2. A Familiar Introduction to the Study of Electricity, 4th Edition, 8vo. 2s. 6d.

3. The History and Present State of Discoveries relating to Vision, Light, and Colours, 2 vols. 4to. illustrated with a great number of Copper-plates, 1l. 11s. 6d. in boards.

4. A Familiar Introduction to the Theory and Practice of Perspective, with Copper-plates, 5s. in boards.

5. Experiments and Observations on different kinds of Air, with Copper-plates, 3 vols. 18s. in boards.

6. Experiments and Observations relating to various branches of Natural Philosophy, with a continuation of the Experiments on Air, price 7s. in boards.

7. Philosopical Empiricism; containing Remarks on a Charge of Plagiarism respecting Dr. H———s, interspersed with various Observations relating to different kinds of Air, 1s. 6d.

8. Directions for impregnating Water with Fixed Air, in order to communicate to it the peculiar Spirit and Virtues of Pyrmont-Water, and other Mineral Waters of a similar Nature, 1s.

N. B. The two preceding Pamphlets are included in No. 5.

9. A New Chart of History; containing a View of the principal Revolutions of Empire that have taken place in the World: with a Book describing it, containing an Epitome of Universal History: 4th Edition, 10s. 6d.

10. A Chart of Biography, with a Book, containing an Explanation of it, and a Catalogue of all the Names inserted in it, 6th Edition, very much improved, 10s. 6d.

11. The Rudiments of English Grammar, adapted to the Use of Schools. 1s. 6d.

12. The above Grammar with Notes and Observations, for the Use of those who have made some Proficiency in the Language. 4th Edition, 3s.

13. Observations relating to Education, more especially as it respects the conduct of the Mind. To which is added, an Essay on a Course of liberal Education for Civil and Active Life, with Plans of Lectures on, 1. The Study of History and General Policy. 2. The History of England. 3. The Constitution and Laws of England. 4s. sewed.

BOOKS written by Dr. PRIESTLEY.

14. A COURSE of LECTURES on ORATORY and CRITICISM, 4to. 10s. 6d. in boards.

15. An ESSAY on the First Principles of GOVERNMENT, and on the Nature of Political, Civil, and Religious LIBERTY, 2d Edition, much enlarged, 4s. sewed.

16. An EXAMINATION of Dr. REID's Inquiry into the Human Mind, on the Principles of Common Sense, Dr. BEATTIE's Essay on the Nature and Immutability of Truth, and Dr. OSWALD's Appeal to Common Sense in behalf of Religion, 2d Edition, 5s. sewed.

17. HARTLEY's THEORY of the HUMAN MIND, on the Principle of the Association of Ideas, with Essays relating to the subject of it, 8vo. 5s. sewed.

18. DISQUISITIONS relating to MATTER and SPIRIT. To which is added, The History of the Philosophical Doctrine concerning the Origin of the Soul, and the Nature of Matter; with its Influence on Christianity, especially with respect to the Doctrine of the Pre-existence of Christ. Also, the DOCTRINE of PHILOSOPHICAL NECESSITY illustrated. 2 vols. 8vo. sewed, 8s. 6d.

19. A FREE DISCUSSION of the DOCTRINES of MATERIALISM and PHILOSOPHICAL NECESSITY, in a Correspondence between Dr. PRICE and Dr. PRIESTLEY. To which are added, by Dr. PRIESTLEY, an INTRODUCTION, explaining the Nature of the Controversy, and Letters to several Writers who have animadverted on his Disquisitions relating to Matter and Spirit, or his Treatise on Necessity. 8vo. 6s. sewed.

20. INSTITUTES of NATURAL and REVEALED RELIGION, Vol. I. containing the Elements of Natural Religion; to which is prefixed, an Essay on the best method of communicating religious Knowledge to the Members of Christian Societies, 2s. 6d. —Vol. II. containing the Evidences of the Jewish and Christian Revelations, 3s. sewed.—Vol. III. containing the Doctrines of Revelation, 2s. 6d. sewed.

21. A HARMONY of the EVANGELISTS, in Greek: To which are prefixed, CRITICAL DISSERTATIONS, in English. 4to. 14s. in boards.

N. B. In the press, and speedily will be published, an *English Harmony*, with an occasional paraphrase, and notes; to which will be added, a Letter to the Bishop of Ossory, in answer to his objections to the principles of this Harmony.

22. A FREE ADDRESS to PROTESTANT DISSENTERS, on the Subject of the Lord's Supper, 3d Edition, with Additions, 2s.

23. The Additions to the above may be had alone, 1s.

24. An ADDRESS to PROTESTANT DISSENTERS, on the Subject of giving the Lord's Supper to Children, 1s.

25. CONSIDERATIONS on DIFFERENCES of OPINION among Christians; with a Letter to the Rev. Mr. VENN, in Answer to his Examination of the Address to Protestant Dissen-

BOOKS written by Dr. PRIESTLEY.

26. A CATECHISM for *Children* or *Young Persons*, 3d Edit. 3d.

27. A SCRIPTURE CATECHISM, consisting of a series of questions, and references to the Scriptures, instead of answers, 3d.

28. A SERIOUS ADDRESS to MASTERS of FAMILIES, with Forms of Family Prayer, 2d Edition, 6d.

29. A VIEW of the PRINCIPLES and CONDUCT of the PROTESTANT DISSENTERS, with respect to the Civil and Ecclesiastical Constitution of England, 2d Edition, 1s. 6d.

30. A FREE ADDRESS to PROTESTANT DISSENTERS, on the Subject of CHURCH DISCIPLINE; with a Preliminary Discourse concerning the Spirit of Christianity, and the Corruption of it by false Notions of Religion, 2s. 6d.

31. A SERMON preached before the Congregation of PROTESTANT DISSENTERS, at Mill-Hill Chapel in Leeds, May 16, 1773, on occasion of his resigning his Pastoral Office among them, 1s.

32. The DOCTRINE of DIVINE INFLUENCE on the Human Mind considered. Price 1s.

33. A FREE ADDRESS to PROTESTANT DISSENTERS, as such. By a Dissenter. A New Edition, enlarged and corrected, 1s. 6d. —An allowance is made to those who buy this Pamphlet to give away.

34. LETTERS to the Author of *Remarks on several late Publications relative to the Dissenters*, in a Letter to Dr. Priestley, 1s.

35. An APPEAL to the serious and candid Professors of Christianity, on the following subjects, viz. 1. The Use of Reason in Matters of Religion. 2. The Power of Man to do the Will of God. 3. Original Sin. 4. Election and Reprobation. 5. The Divinity of Christ: and, 6. Atonement for Sin by the Death of Christ, 5th Edtition, 1d.

36. A Familiar Illustration of certain Passages of Scripture relating to the same subject, 4d. or 3s. 6d. per dozen.

37. The TRIUMPH of TRUTH; being an Account of the Trial of Mr. Elwall for Heresy and Blasphemy, at Stafford Assizes, before Judge Denton, 2d Edition, 1d.

38. CONSIDERATIONS for the Use of YOUNG MEN, and the Parents of YOUNG MEN, 2d Edition, 2d.

Also, Published under the Direction of Dr. PRIESTLEY,

THE THEOLOGICAL REPOSITORY: Consisting of Original Essays, Hints, Queries, &c. calculated to promote religious Knowledge, in Three Volumes, 8vo. Price 18s. in boards.

In the First Volume, which is now re-printed, several Articles are added, particularly Two Letters from Dr. THOMAS SHAW to Dr. BENSON, relating to the Passage of the Israelites through the Red Sea.

A SECOND LETTER

TO THE

Rev. Mr. JOHN PALMER, &c.

[Price Six-Pence.]

A SECOND LETTER

TO

The Rev. Mr. JOHN PALMER,

IN DEFENCE OF THE

Doctrine of Philosophical Necessity.

BY

JOSEPH PRIESTLEY, LL. D. F. R. S.

I love to pour out all myself, as plain
As downright Shippen, or as old Montaigne.

POPE.

LONDON:
PRINTED BY H. BALDWIN,
FOR J. JOHNSON, NO. 72, ST. PAUL'S CHURCH-YARD.
M DCC LXXX.

To the Rev. Mr. PALMER.

DEAR SIR,

YOU, as I foretold, have thought proper to reply to my letter, and, as I suspected, *circumstances have determined me* to write you a *second letter*; and my motives have, I suppose, been the same with those that determined you to reply to the first. For I by no means think your reply to be satisfactory, and I am willing to try whether I cannot convince you, or at least our readers, that this opinion is well founded.

Your treatife, I perceive, is deemed to contain the ftrength of the caufe you have efpoufed; and I think I fhould do wrong to fhrink from the difcuffion, while I have any hope of prevailing upon a perfon fo fully equal to it, to canvafs it with me, and while I think there is any reafonable profpect, that, by continuing a friendly controverfy, any of the difficulties attending the fubject may be cleared up. The queftion before us is truely momentous, the arguments that decide in my favour I think to be very plain, your objections appear to me to admit of fufficiently eafy anfwers; and, in my opinion, it is nothing but imaginary confequences, or fuch as are grofsly mifunderftood, at which the mind of any man can revolt.

You, who know me pretty well, will not fay that I would flur over a difficulty by which I was really preffed; and *arrogant* as you may fuppofe me to be, you will think me *fincere,* and that my confidence is derived

rived from a full perfuasion, well or ill founded, on a subject which I have long considered, and with respect to which I have formed so deliberate and decided a judgement.

I shall divide my present letter, as I did my former, into distinct heads, and shall discuss them in what appears to me to be their most natural order. I wish you had divided your *Appendix* in the same manner, as it contributes much to perspicuity, and relieves the attention of the reader.

SECTION I.

Of the stating of the Question.

YOU complain of me for having *misrepresented your meaning*, when what you assert on the occasion, in my opinion, confirms my representation. I said that you supposed the mind capable of determining *contrary to any motive whatever*, or, as I afterwards express it, either *without, or contrary to motives*. You reply, p. 24, " I ne-
" ver said, or supposed, that a rational being
" can act without any motive, good or
" bad; but the most that I ever said was,
" that, in the very same circumstances, in
" which the choice, or determination of
" the mind, was directed to one object of
" pursuit, it might have brought itself to
" will or determine on the pursuit of a
" different and contrary one."
Now

Now where is the real difference between my stating of the case and yours? You say you make choice of one object of pursuit, for which, by your present confession, you must have had *some motive*; and yet might have taken a different and contrary one. But how could you do this, without acting against the motives which led you to prefer the other? If you admit that we never act but with the *strongest* motives, as well as never without *some* motive (and one of these seems to be the necessary consequence of the other) you must, in this case, have acted against the strongest motive. And, if for this possible determination there was no *motive at all* (and if it was overbalanced by other motives, it was, in fact, no motive at all) you must have acted *without* any motive for what you did, as well as *against* motives to the contrary.

Besides, what is the boasted power of *self determination*, if the mind cannot actually determine itself *without* any motive at all, or *contrary* to any motives, at pleasure. If this be not the case, it is very improperly called *self determination.*

SECTION II.

Of CERTAINTY, *or* UNIVERSALITY, *as the Ground of concluding that any Thing is* NECESSARY.

IN order to shew that the distinction between *certainty* and *necessity*, on which you and others lay so much stress, is nothing to your purpose, I observed that all that we mean by *necessity*, in any case, is *the cause of certainty,* or of universality; and that this is applicable to things *corporeal* or *mental*, without distinction; that the reason, and the only reason, why we say a stone falls to the ground *necessarily*, is that it *constantly* and *universally* does so; and therefore that, if the determination of the mind be always according to motives, the difference

DOCTRINE OF NECESSITY.

ference as I said p. 23, cannot be in the *reality*, but in the *kind* of the necessity. " The necessity must be equally strict and " absolute in both cases, let the *causes* of " the necessity by ever so different."

This argument I said you had not given sufficient attention to. But you now tell me, p. 7, " You were so far from over- " looking it, that you regarded it as the " basis on which my argument for the ne- " cessary determination of the mind rested, " but that you considered," p. 8. " that " what you had insisted on to establish the " distinction between physical and moral " necessity, as really replying to this very " argument," and you refer me to p. 49, &c. of your treatise.

Now I have carefully read over those pages, but I am very far from finding in them any thing to justify your reference. Because, admitting the distinction you contend for between *physical* and *moral* necessity, still it is a *necessity*; and if necessity have any meaning at all, it is that, while the laws of nature are what they are, the event denominated necessary *could not have been otherwise.*

You say, p. 50, "We may multiply ever "so many other causes, or circumstances, "concurring with and leading to the choice "that is made, it is plain they can only "operate as *moral*, not as *physical* causes." But to what purpose is the distinction of physical and moral, if they be *real* causes, when all real causes must, in given circumstances, produce real and constant effects?

"They may be," you say, "*occasions*, "or *grounds*, of determination, but they "do not *form*, or *necessitate* the determi- "nation." I will allow your language; but if, in fact, the mind never *does* determine otherwise than according to these same *motives, occasions, or grounds*, there is nothing in any received mode of reasoning that

that will justify you in saying, that the mind, even *could*, in those circumstances, have determined otherwise, or that, according to the present laws of nature respecting the mind, the determination was not, in the strictest sense of the word, *necessary*. For there cannot be any evidence of the existence of a *power* independent of its known *effects*.

In what manner do we prove the existence of *all powers* but by their actual *operation?* Give me, in the whole compass of nature, any other case similar to this of your *self determining power*, that is, a case in which we admit a *real power* without having ever seen its *effects*. All our rules of reasoning in philosophy would be violated by such a proceeding. *Effects* are the only evidences of *powers*, or *causes;* and the immediate consequence of this is, that if no event ever *does* take place, we can have no reason to believe that it *can* take place. This is as easily applicable to the case before

fore us as any whatever. Produce a case in which the mind indisputably *determines itself* without any motive whatever, and then, *but then only*, shall I admit that motives have no necessary influence over its determination.

I must still maintain, therefore, that you have given no answer at all to my argument for the doctrine of necessity, as inferred from the consideration of *constancy* and *universality*.

There is, I repeat it, just the same propriety in calling the determinations of the mind, as there is in calling the falling of a stone, *necessary*. It is not the *same law*, or power, in nature, that causes both, and therefore they may be distinguished by what names you please; but they equally *ensure the event*; and the course of nature must be changed before the results, in either case, can be otherwise than they are observed to be.

SECTION III.

SECTION III.

Of the Consequence of admitting the CER-
TAINTY *of Determination.*

WHAT you reply to my observations concerning *certainty*, and the several distinctions of it, is so manifestly unsatisfactory, that I must beg leave to recall your attention to the argument. I asserted that if the determination of the mind be, in any proper sense of the word, *certain*, all the same consequences, even the very frightful ones that you describe, will follow, just as on the supposition of its being *necessary*; for that, in this case, the two words cannot but mean the very same thing.

You now acknowledge, p. 9, " that mo-
" ral certainty may be a real one, though
" not

" not physical," and, p. 8, " that certainty
" is as different as the different causes or
" occasions of it." Now I really cannot see what these differences (which I will admit to be as many as you please) can signify; if, as you allow, the result, is invariably the same. This is certainly a case to which you cannot have given sufficient attention, or you could not treat it so lightly as you do. I shall, therefore *open*, and *expand* it a little for you, to give you an opportunity of seeing more distinctly what it is that you *do* admit, when you allow, under whatever distinction you please, that the determination of the mind is *certain*, or, in other words, *definite in definite circumstances*.

Every man, you must allow, is born with a certain constitution of body and mind, intirely independent of his own choice. The circumstances in which he is born, with respect to country, parents, education, and advantages or disadvantages
of

of all kinds, are, likewife altogether independent of himfelf. It is no matter when, you fay, that *his firft proper volition* takes place, for you muft admit it is, in *certain definite circumftances*, independent of himfelf. His determination, therefore, being by the hypothefis, *certain*, or *definite* in thofe circumftances, whatever it be, it brings him into other, but definite, circumftances; whether forefeen or unforefeen by himfelf depends upon his judgment or fagacity. In thefe new circumftances, he makes another *definite choice*, or determination, concerning the *new objects* that are now before him; and this new determination brings him into other new circumftances. And thus his whole life paffes in a conftant fucceffion of *circumftances* and *determinations*, all infeparably connected, till you come to the laft determination of all, immediately preceeding the extinction of all his powers by death.

Now it is obvious to afk, if all this be really *certain*, one thing ftrictly depending

ing upon another; so that there is never known to be any variation from it, in what does it, or *can* it, differ from what is contended for by the necessarian. If I know my own principles, it is all that I want, call it by what name you please. You happen to like the word *certain*, whereas I prefer the word *necessary*; but our ideas *must* be the very same. We both chalk out a *definite path* for every man to walk in, from the commencement of his life to the termination of it. The path is the same, drawn by the same line, and by the same rule. It is a path that you admit no man ever gets out of; and this, I do assure you, is all that I mean, if I know my own meaning, when I say he never *can* get out of it: for the laws of his nature must be changed, so that his determinations must (contrary to the present hypothesis) not be definite in definite circumstances, before he *can* get out of it, from his birth to his death.

But

But you say, p. 9, "the power of agency "still remains, if the certainty with which "he acts be only a *moral* certainty, where- "as by that which is *physical* it is destroy- "ed." But if you reflect a moment, you will perceive, that this is inconsistent with what you just before granted. Because if, in any case, the determination *might have been* otherwise than it is, it would not have been *certain,* but *contingent.* Certainty undoubtedly excludes all *possible variety,* for that implies *uncertainty.* Besides, as I observed before, and I cannot repeat it too often, till I ensure your attention to it, what *proof* or *evidence* can you produce of the reality or existence of any *power,* that is never exerted. If, therefore, you allow that all determinations whatever are certain, being directed by motives, what evidence can there be of a power to act contrary to motives?

How unreasonable, then, is it to reply, as you do, p. 13, to your child " Do not
" you,

"you, my son, see a vast difference between "determining yourself, call it *certainly*, "if you please, and being *necessarily* deter- "mined by something else." Because knowing the *absolute certainty* (though not necessity) of his determination, in the circumstances in which you placed him, you should not have placed him in them, unless you really *chose* that he should make the determination that you knew he *certainly would* make; and therefore, on your own maxims, you would do wrong to *blame*, or *punish* him.

You ask him whether "he was not con- "scious he had a power of refusing the "apples;" whereas, by your own confession, that power could not possibly be *exerted*, so as to be of any *use* to him, but on the supposition of what you previously knew did not exist, viz. *a different disposition of mind*, in consequence of which his love of apples would have been less, or his fear of punishment greater, than you *knew* it to be.

SECTION IV.

SECTION IV.

Of the supposed Consciousness of Liberty.

I Desired you to attend to the *phenomena of human nature*, to consider whether it be not a *fact*, that human volitions depend upon the previous disposition of their minds and the circumstances in which they are placed, in order to determine whether their volitions are not invariably *according to those circumstances;* and therefore whether, in propriety of language, it should not be said that they are always, and necessarily, determined by those circumstances, or motives. You reply, p. 22, " if the phenomena of
" human nature are to determine the ques-
" tion, we must certainly include the
" *whole* phenomena, one of which is, that
" let

"let actions be ever so definite in definite circumstances, they are still conscious of having it in their power to determine otherwise than they actually did," now I am surprised that you should not have been aware, that this is directly inconsistent with your own supposition, viz. the determination being *definite*; for if it might have been *otherwise*, it would have been *indefinite*. No man can be conscious of an *impossibility*. If, therefore, the real phenomena, exclusive of all pretended consciousness, are in favour of our volitions being definite, all *possibility* of their being indefinite is necessarily excluded; so that they could not have been different from what they actually are, in any given circumstances.

Besides, reflect a little what is it of which we *can* be conscious; for consciousness has its limits, as well as other things. It is not that, with the same disposition of mind and in the same circumstances, the determination

mination might have been different. This is a manifest fallacy. All that, in the nature of things, we *can* be conscious of, is that had we been differently disposed, we might have acted differently; that nothing but our own *will*, or pleasure, prevented our acting differently; which you know is not at all contrary to any thing contended for by necessarians. Consider particularly my *Additional Illustrations*, p. 286, &c.

SECTION V.

Of the Difference between the WILL *and the* JUDGMENT.

IN the passage to which you have now referred me, in your former treatise, p. 50, you lay great stress on the essential difference between the nature of the *will*, and that of the *judgment*. " The will, you say, " implies

"implies, in its very nature, a freedom from all controlling necessary influence. It is the power of *self determination* belonging to an agent, the physical independency of which on any thing foreign to itself makes it to be what it is, or constitutes its very essence. The different mode of operation belonging to the will," p. 52, "as distinct from the other faculties of the mind, arises out of its different nature. The will is an independent, active principle, or faculty. The other faculties are dependent and merely passive, &c."

Now I rather wonder that, in all this loftiness of language, you should not have perceived, that you are taking for granted the very thing in dispute. If we judge of the *powers* and faculties of man by his *actions* (and *what can we reason but from what we know)* we must conclude that he is *not* possessed of any such faculty as you describe. On the contrary, we see all men without

without exception, driven to and fro, juft as their circumftances and motives impel them, without ever once exerting (as far as appears) a fingle act of proper *felf determination*. In all cafes of fufficient magnitude, and in which there is fufficient opportunity given us to examine them, we fee very plainly, that men are actuated by very *determinate motives*; and we are here, as in other fimilar cafes, authorized to judge of obfcure cafes by thofe which are more diftinct and evident, of the fame kind.

Befides, fo far am I from perceiving any fuch effential *difference* as you defcribe between the *will* and the *judgment*, that I perceive a remarkable *refemblance* between them, and in that very refpect in which you ftate them to differ the moft. Does the judgment decide according to the appearance of objects? So does the will; and if we confult fact, in no other way; infomuch, that the *will itfelf*, exclufive of the *actions*, or *motions*, that follow the will, may not be improperly called a *particular judgment*, deciding on the *preferableness* of objects, according to their appearances, which are often very deceitful. For, judging by whatever *rule* you please, whatever object, at the moment of determination, appears *preferable*, that we always chuse. If, therefore, as I have said before, there be a power of self determination in the will, I should expect to find the same in the judgment also, and if you will distinguish them, in the judgment preferably to the will; if that may be called *judgment* which *decides*, tho' concerning the *preferableness* of objects. And there is no reason why this should not be the province of judgment, properly so called, as well as that of deciding concerning the *truth* of objects.

You object to the conclusiveness of my reasoning, p. 18, to prove that from one of your arguments it would follow that *judgment* and *volition* were the same thing, and the same with the *circulation of the blood*,

blood, &c. suppofing that it goes on the idea of judgment being an *act* of the mind, only in the popular fenfe of the word. Now I will fhew you that my inference was truly drawn, independent of any fuch definition of the word, as will appear by leaving out the word *act* altogether. You will then fay, p. 80, " Can that be truly faid to be my *volition*, which is produced by *fomething over which I had no power*. On that ground, every thing that takes place in my *body*, as well as in my *mind*, may, with equal propriety, be called my vo- lition; and fo the *circulation of the blood*, and the *pulfation of the heart*, may, with equal reafon, be called my volitions."

The medium of your proof, or the *middle term* in your fyllogifm, is not *an act*, but *fomething over which we have no power*. But, though the *circulation of the blood*, &c. fhould, upon the doctrine of neceffity, agree with *volition*, in being *a thing over which we have no power*, it does not, in that refpect, respect, agree with *volition only*, but with *judgment* also, and every other affection of the mind.

I may perhaps make the inconclusiveness of your argument more apparent, by reducing it to the form of a *syllogism*, and framing another exactly similar to it. Your argument will then stand as follows. "According to "the necessarians,

"Volition is a thing over which a man "has no power.
"But the pulsation of the heart is a "thing over which a man has no "power.
"*Ergo*, The pulsation of the heart is a "volition."

A syllogism exactly parallel to this of yours is the following:

A goose is an animal that has two feet.
But a man is an animal that has two feet.
Ergo, A man is a goose.

But

I am forry to have occafion to recall to your attention the firft principles of logick, but it is plain you had overlooked them, when you thought you had reduced the neceffarian to acknowledge that, on his principles, the *circulation of the blood*, and the *pulfation of the heart*, muft be termed *volitions*. You meant to turn our principles into ridicule, and muft take the confequence if the ridicule rebound upon yourfelf. You certainly had the merit of attempting fomething *new* in this, but there is always fome *hazard* in attempting novelties.

SECTION VI.

SECTION VI.

Of the Argument from the supposed CONSEQUENCES *of the Doctrine of Necessity.*

TO my objection to your reasoning from the *consequences* of the doctrine of necessity, you reply, p. 4, "There are con-"sequences that seem greatly to out weigh "all speculative reasonings of every sort "which can be thought of, and incon-"testably prove that the doctrine which "such consequences attend is not and "cannot be, true." You add, that Dr. Watts recommends the mode of arguing from consequences, and that I myself have adopted it.

Now this, sir, you do without making proper *distinctions*, which Dr. Watts, in the

the very passage which you have quoted, might have taught you to make. He says, that "the false proposition must be re- futed by shewing that an evident *false- hood*, or *absurdity*, will follow from it," which is the very thing that I did, when I shewed that, in consequence of ad- mitting your doctrine of liberty, you must suppose that *effects* take place without *ade- quate causes*, and that the Divine Being could have no prescience of human actions, which the scriptures every where suppose. On the other hand, the consequences that you draw from the doctrine of necessity only relate to things that you *dislike*, and *abhor*, and which have nothing to do with *truth*.

Shew me that any *falsehood*, or *absur- dity*, as Dr. Watts says, follows from the doctrine of necessity, and I shall not then say, that we must *acquiesce* in it, and *make the best we can* of it. For it is absolutely im- possible to acquiesce in an acknowledged falsehood

falsehood, as we may in a thing that we merely cannot *relish*. With respect to all things that merely exite *disgust*, besides that it may be conceived, that the disgust may be *ill founded* (and in this case it appears to me to be manifestly so) it is well known that there are many *truths*, and valuable ones too, that are *ungrateful*, especially at the first proposal.

Now I challenge you to shew that any proper *falsehood*, or *absurdity*, will follow from the principles of necessity, a thing that I *do* pretend to with respect to the doctrine of liberty. And do not any more say, as you do now, p. 6, that " it is in " the same way of reasoning with that " which I have used," that you have endeavoured to support the doctrine of liberty. By this time, I hope, you see there is a great difference between the two cases.

SECTION VII.

SECTION VII.

Of the MORAL INFLUENCE *of the Doctrine of Necessity.*

YOU complain, but very unjustly, of my mode of reasoning, when I endeavour to undermine all that you have urged on the subject of the *dangerous consequences* of the doctrine of necessity. Your meaning, you say, p. 17, was " that it tends to in-
" dispose a person for virtuous activity,
" and self command, but that you sup-
" pose the necessarian to be active enough
" in gratifying his irregular and vicious
" inclinations." Now I had no doubt of your *willingness* to make a distinction in this case, that is, to make the necessarian *indolent to good,* and at the same time *active*

to evil; but nature, not being of the party, makes no such distinction; so that the case you suppose is an impossibility.

If the belief of the doctrine of necessity has any operation at all, either to *activity,* or *inactivity,* it must respect all *ends,* or *objects, as such,* and without distinction, whatever they be, and can never operate one way if a man's inclinations be virtuous, and another way if they be vicious. If on the one hand, I believe that my object will be accomplished, and my belief lead me to *overlook all means,* and therefore I give myself no trouble about it; or if, on the other, my belief of the necessary connection of means and ends be such as that my exertions are redoubled; still these different consequences respect *all objects alike,* and can never operate to the disadvantage of virtue, but on the supposition that all necessarians, *as such,* either are more indifferent to their own happiness than other men, or have less knowledge of the necessary

DOCTRINE OF NECESSITY.

fary connection between virtue and happinefs.

(If this was the cafe, furely you might, confidering the length of time that has elapfed fince the doctrine of neceffity was firft propofed by Mr. Hobbes, and even fince it has been fully eftablifhed, as I may fay, by Dr. Hartley (and before my recollection, or yours, it had numerous advocates among men of letters) have been able to collect fomething like *pofitive evidence;* and you certainly fhould not have raifed all this outcry without fome better foundation than your own fufpicious *imagination.*

SECTION VIII.

SECTION VIII.

Miscellaneous Observations.

YOU eagerly catch, p. 27, at a casual, and as you think, an improper expression of mine, when I said that "the origin "of action, or of self determination, is "the same as the origin of the deity, con- "cerning which we know nothing at all," as if I really supposed the deity to have had an origin, or a beginning. Whereas, besides that you well know that I suppose, just as much as yourself, that the deity is properly *uncaused*, and consequently had *no origin*, and therefore that it *could* be no more than an inadvertent expression that you had got hold of, I have, in fact, said the same thing in this very place, viz. that proper action, or self determination, can have no beginning, because it must have commenced with the deity, who had none. This triumph yours, of which you seem willing to make so much, is, indeed premature.

If, in maintaining an opinion common to myself and Dr. Price, I should have said, that " the commencement of the creation " was the same with that of the deity him- " self;" would not the obvious construction have been, not that they both had a beginning, but that *neither* of them had any? In this case, also, I am just as far from intimating, in the most distant manner, that it was even *possible* for the deity to have had any *origin*. I must say that this construction of my words is very extraordinary.

You charge me, p. 33, with having mis-stated Dr. Price's opinion on the subject of liberty, as well as your own; but, though I am not sensible of having made any mistake in this respect, it is not a point that I choose to discuss with *you*. It is sufficient for my present purpose, if I truly state,

state, and fully refute, *your* opinion on the subject.

Here you must give me leave to observe, that it was very improper, on several accounts, to add the name of Dr. Price to those of Locke, Wollaston, Clarke, and Foster, as authorities in favour of the doctrine of liberty, for whom I ought to have had a *greater reverence*. I also could muster up a list of very respectable authorities, such as Collins, Leibnitz, Hutcheson, Edwards, Hartley, &c. but, for obvious reasons, I should have chosen to have confined it to the *dead*, and should have omitted the *living*, especially the man with whom my antagonist had a public and truly amicable controversy on the subject. Dr. Price, however, I am well persuaded, believes that my respect for him is not less than yours, notwithstanding I may imagine that his eye, though much stronger than mine, is not able to see through some little *cloud* that happens to hang between it and this particular subject.

Were

Were I to set about it, I should not doubt but that, though I cannot say *nos turba sumus*, I could draw out a very decent list of *living authorities* in favour of the doctrine of necessity, consisting of persons whose *ability*, *virtue*, and I will add *activity* too, you would not question. And were we to leave out those who would not pretend to have properly *studied* the subject, and therefore could not be said to give a vote, except by *proxy*, my list, among men of letters, might perhaps be not only as *respectable*, but even as *numerous* as yours. But this is a question that is not to be decided by *vote* or *authority*, but by *argument*; and it is on this ground that we are now engaged.

D 2   SECTION IX.

SECTION IX.

Queries addressed to Mr. PALMER.

THUS, Sir, I have diſtinctly replied to every thing that I imagine yourſelf can think *material* in your *Appendix*, in which you ſay you have " noticed " thoſe parts of my Letter to you which " were deemed moſt material." Now, as you would not have *voluntarily* undertaken the diſcuſſion of this argument with me, without having well weighed your force in it, and being determined to bring it to ſomething more like a proper *cloſe*; I hope that, notwithſtanding you ſay you ſhall now " decline the controverſy," you will, on more mature conſideration, *reſume* it, and give me, as the Spectator pleaſantly ſays, *more laſt words of Richard Baxter.* I ſhall

shall therefore tell you what I think you have omitted, and what it behoved you more particularly to have replied to in my *Letter*. And, farther, to make the *continuation* of the correspondence more easy to you, I shall state those matters in distinct *queries,* to which, if you please, you may reply in order.

1. You had said that a determination of the mind is not *an effect without a cause*, though it be not produced by any motive, because the *self-determining power itself* is the cause. I replied, that, allowing this supposed power to be the cause of *choice in general*, it can no more be considered as the cause of any *particular choice*, than the *motion of the air* in general can be said to be the cause of any particular *wind*; because all winds are equally motions of the air, and therefore, that there must be some *farther cause* of any particular wind. I desire you to point out the insufficiency of this answer. This it the more behoves you to do, because

cause it respects not the *outworks*; but the very *inmost retreat* of your doctrine of liberty. If you cannot defend yourself against this attack, you must surrender at discretion. Necessity, with all its *horrid consequences*, will enter in at the breach; and you know that necessarians, though slothful to good, are active enough in mischief, and give no quarter.

That you should say you had not passed over any thing of *the argumentative kind* in my *Letter*, which seemed to require a reply, and yet have overlooked this most material article, as well as many others, surprises me not a little.

On this subject, I also beg you would not fail to give particular attention to the fifth article of my *Additional Illustrations*, printed in the *correspondence with Dr. Price*, p. 288, in which, I think I have proved decisively, that the *mind itself* can never be considered as a proper and sufficient cause of *particular determinations*.

It

DOCTRINE OF NECESSITY. 39

It was unfortunate for these *Illustrations*, that they did not appear till after the greatest part of your first treatise was written, and yet so long before your *appendix*, that I suppose they were forgotten. Though, as you had seen them before you wrote the *preface*, and consequently some time before the publication of your first piece, you had a good opportunity of animadverting upon them, and might be expected to do it in a case that so materially affected your main argument.

You now say, in general, that " now " I have read them, they appear as little " satisfactory as the former; and that to " all which Dr. Priestley has advanced in " the correspondence, Dr. Price appears " to have given a very clear and sufficient " reply." But this particular article, not being a proper part of the correspondence, you will find, that Dr. Price has not replied to it at all, and therefore your answer to it is not precluded. I particularly

intreat

intreat you to refute what is there advanced. Point out to me any thing in *your work*, which you think I have not sufficiently considered, and I promise to be as particular in my discussion of it as you please.

‘ 2. I endeavoured to shew, in my second Section, that the argument from the consideration of cause and effect does not, as you say, go on the supposition of *a similarity of the constituent principles of matter and spirit*, but only on the determination of the mind being subject to *any laws at all*; and therefore that the cause of liberty can derive no advantage from the commonly received principles of the *immateriality of the human soul*. You should have said, whether my reply was satisfactory to you, or not. But perhaps I am to interpret your *silence* on any subject to be an *acquiescence* in what I observed concerning it, and not as an article that you thought too obviously inconclusive to demand any reply.

3. Please

3. Please to produce some direct proof of the existence of the *self-determining power* you boast so much of. I mean a proof from *fact*, and not from a merely imagined *feeling*, or *consciousness* of it, which one person may assert, and another, who is certainly constituted in the same manner, may deny. What I assert is, that all we *can feel*, or be *conscious of*, in the case, is that our actions, corporeal or mental, depend upon our *will*, or *pleasure*; but to say that our wills are not always influenced by *motives*, is so far from being *agreeable*, that it is directly *contrary* to all experience in ourselves, and all observation of others.

4. You have said nothing to explain, or soften your denial of the doctrine of *divine prescience*, which, as a *christian*, and a *christian minister*, it greatly behoves you to do. You pretend to be shocked at the consequences of the doctrine of necessity, which exist only in your own imagination; but here is a consequence of your doctrine of

of liberty, directly repugnant to the whole tenor of revelation, as it has been understood by all who have ever pretended to any faith in it, though they have differed ever so much in other things. It will be well worth your while to make *another appendix* to your book, if it were only to give some little *plausibility* to this business, and either to shew, if you can, that the divine prescience is not a doctrine of the scriptures, or that the sacred writers were mistaken with respect to it. Besides, it is incumbent upon you to shew, independent of your profession as a christian, how, on your own principles, any such *government of the world* as we see to take place could exist. To say, as you do, that God, notwithstanding his want of prescience, may yet govern free beings in the best manner that free beings *can* be governed, will avail you nothing; because I maintain, that if liberty be what you define it to be, a power of *proper self-determination*, such beings cannot be governed at all.

all. I have shewn that it is impossible they should ever be proper subjects of moral government. The Divine Being cannot controul their actions; the influence of all motives (the only instruments of moral government) will be altogether uncertain; he can form no judgment of their effect; and, in consequence, all must be anarchy and confusion.

But I would rather advise you to *retract* what you have too hastily advanced. If possible, think of some method of reconciling *prescience* with *liberty*; and by no means purchase your liberty at so very great a price. At least be *very sure*, in the first place, that it is worth so much.

If, as I suppose will be the case, you should not be able to reconcile *prescience* with your more favourite doctrine of *free-will*, be advised by me, rather than give up the former so lightly as you do, to keep it *at all events*; even though, in order to

do

do it, you should be obliged to rank it (as many truly pious christians do the doctrines of *transubstantiation* and the *Trinity*) among the *mysteries of faith*, things to be held sacred, and not to be submitted to rational inquiry. On no account would I abandon such a doctrine as that of *Divine prescience*, while I retained the least respect for revelation, or wished to look with any satisfaction on the moral government under which I live.

Lest you should think all this to be nothing more than affected seriousness, and the language of a mere controversialist, pushing his adversary on a precipice, I shall quote what a brother of yours in this very controversy with me observes; and it is no less a person than the celebrated Mr. Bryant. And when he (after Dr. Price and yourself) shall have advanced all that he is able, I should think the public will be satisfied that the most ample justice must have been done to that side of the question,

Speaking

Speaking of those who scruple not to give up the doctrine of *divine prescience,* rather than abandon that of *liberty,* he says, in his *Address to me,* p. 36, "They must then give up the *scriptures* at the same time, and with the scriptures, their *religion* and *faith.* For in the sacred writings the foreknowledge of the deity is not only inculcated as a *doctrine,* but proved by a variety of *events.*"—If, sir, the earnest language of what you may suppose (though very unjustly) to be *enmity* fail to move you, let that of *friendship* prevail.

If after this repeated warning, you should persist in treating the doctrine of divine prescience as a thing of so little consequence, the most truly *candid* thing I can say is what you have quoted, and endeavoured to expose, as the extreme of *uncharitableness* when first advanced in my controversy with Dr. Beattie, on the same occasion. But because you may think the figurative expression too strong (though, in fact, the stronger it is

the

the better apology it makes) I shall say the same thing in other words. "It is what "the heat of disputation has betrayed you "into. You are blind to the consequences, "and therefore *you know not what you do.*"

5. I particularly desire you would once more go over with me the subject of the *practical influence* of the doctrine of necessity. This is far from being, in my opinion, the *dark* side of my argument. I love, and rejoice in this view of it; confident, and I hope I may add, *feeling,* that, when rightly understood, it is highly favourable to every thing that is great and good in man. Tell me whether the belief of the certainty of the end, *without* any idea of the necessary connection of the means by which it is brought about (which is the doctrine of *Calvinism*) does not work one way, and the belief of the certainty of the end, only *as a consequence* of its necessary connection with the previous means (which is the doctrine of *philosophical necessity)*

does

does not work another way. Re-peruse my account of their different influences, and shew, from a juster view of the principles of human nature, that, with those apprehensions, men must feel and act differently from what I have supposed they naturally would do.

6. I likewise desire you would particularly attend to what I have observed in my seventh section, with respect to the use of the term *agency* and *responsibility*; because, if what I have there observed be just, you, and other defenders of the doctrine of liberty can derive no advantage whatever from any argument in which it is taken for granted, that man, in your sense of the terms, is an *agent*, and a *responsible* being; as I shew, that the state of moral government in which we are, is perfectly consistent with, nay, pre-supposes the doctrine of necessity; that for this purpose it is sufficient that man be, in the popular sense of the word only, and not in a sense that pre-

supposes

supposes the doctrine of liberty, an *agent*, and *responsible*. Nay, I beg you would shew how man, constituted as you suppose him to be, can be a subject of moral government at all.

7. As you lay great stress on the feeling of *remorse*, I beg you would consider, and reply to what I have urged on that subject, in my letter to you, p. 62, and my *additional illustrations*, p. 296. If my state of the fact be just, no argument from that topic can avail you any thing; every just view of that subject being extremely favourable, rather than unfavourable, to the doctrine of necessity.

Please to observe that all these queries relate to matters strictly *argumentative*, or that must be allowed to have weight in forming our judgment on the subject in debate; and do not pass them over a second time, as if they were things of *another nature*, and such as you are under no obligation

gation to notice. Say, if you pleafe, and *prove* it, if you can, that what I have advanced with refpect to them is *inconclufive;* but do not pafs them over in filence, as if they were not of an *argumentative* nature, or indeed, not very *materially* fo.

THE CONCLUSION.

Dear Sir,

I Do not know that it is neceffary for me to call your attention particularly to any other points in conteft between us; but I earneftly beg your explicit reply to thefe few. Many controverfies have terminated without effect, and without any advantage to the caufe of truth, merely becaufe the parties have not come to a fair *iffue*, but have left their readers wifhing to know what the one or the other of them would have replied to this or that argument, or to this

this or that state, or view of it. I wish to carry this controversy to its *proper conclusion*. For my part, I will readily answer any question you shall think proper to propose to me, and shall do it without the least reserve or evasion. You *believe* that I would. I only beg that you would, in like manner, reply to me. More, I think, is to be done by distinct *interrogatories*, and categorical *answers*, than in any other manner. Let us, however, try this method. A very few more short pieces, which, with what we have already published, would not make too bulky *a single volume* for each of us, might, I think, exhaust all that we can now have to say that is material. Why then, when the trouble will be so little, and the advantage may be so great, should you decline this business prematurely? You have certainly as much *leisure* for the discussion as I have; and as it was you that called me out, and not I that called upon you, I should imagine you have not less *zeal* in the cause than myself.

You cannot apprehend from me any thing offensive to you in my manner of writing, any more than I can with respect to you; nor shall I take offence at *little things*. You may make what reflections you please on my *temper* or *manner*, and there are points enow to hit in both, if you be so disposed. You have my leave beforehand, to say that I am *insolent* in one place, and *arrogant* in another; and you may parody my most obnoxious paragraphs, whether *in* the work you are answering, or *out of it*, if it will serve to amuse yourself or your readers. If there be more of pleasantry than ill-nature in your strictures, I will chearfully bear it all, and with Themistocles to Pausanias, say, *strike me*, and as often as you please, *but hear me*, and answer me.

Whatever I *have been*, or may be to *others, you* shall have nothing to complain of with respect to *yourself personally*; and I am so happy to find myself engaged with a person a person of undoubted judgment in the controversy, that, I own, I am very unwilling to part with you so soon. I shall be like Horace's friend, and you must have recourse to as many shifts to get quit of me.

Hoping, therefore, to have the satisfaction of hearing from you again on the subject, and wishing your reply may be as speedy as will be consistent with its being *well weighed,* I am,

DEAR SIR,

Your very humble servant,

J. PRIESTLEY.

Calne, April 1780.

www.ingramcontent.com/pod-product-compliance
Lightning Source LLC
Chambersburg PA
CBHW030301170426
43202CB00009B/832